KV-638-900

DISCARD
BIRMINGHAM LIBRARY SERVICES

Divorce and Separation

Rosy Border & Jane Moir

BIRMINGHAM LIBRARIES/BIB SERVICES	
Cypher	23.02.04
346.42016	12.95

Cavendish
Publishing
Limited

London • Sydney • Portland, Oregon

Second edition first published in Great Britain 2004 by
Cavendish Publishing Limited, The Glass House,
Wharton Street, London WC1X 9PX, United Kingdom
Telephone: + 44 (0)20 7278 8000   Facsimile: + 44 (0)20 7278 8080
Email: info@cavendishpublishing.com
Website: www.cavendishpublishing.com

Published in the United States by Cavendish Publishing
c/o International Specialized Book Services,
5824 NE Hassalo Street, Portland,
Oregon 97213-3644, USA

Published in Australia by Cavendish Publishing (Australia) Pty Ltd
45 Beach Street, Coogee, NSW 2034, Australia
Email: info@cavendishpublishing.com.au
Website: www.cavendishpublishing.com.au

© Border, Rosy and Moir, Jane   2004

The first edition of this title was previously published by The Stationery Office

All rights reserved. No part of this publication may be reproduced, stored in a
retrieval system, or transmitted, in any form or by any means, electronic, mechanical,
photocopying, recording, scanning or otherwise, without the prior permission in
writing of Cavendish Publishing Limited, or as expressly permitted by law, or under
the terms agreed with the appropriate reprographics rights organisation. Enquiries
concerning reproduction outside the scope of the above should be sent to the
Rights Department, Cavendish Publishing Limited, at the address above.

You must not circulate this book in any other binding or cover
and you must impose the same condition on any acquirer.

British Library Cataloguing in Publication Data
Border, Rosy
Divorce and separation – 2nd ed – (Pocket lawyer)
1 Divorce – Law and legislation – England 2 Divorce – Law
and legislation – Wales
I Title II Moir, Jane III Border, Rosy Divorce
346.4'20166

Library of Congress Cataloguing in Publication Data
Data available

ISBN 1-85941-862-7

1 3 5 7 9 10 8 6 4 2

Printed and bound in Great Britain

Contents

Disclaimer

This book puts *you* in control. This is an excellent thing, but it also makes *you* responsible for using it properly. Few washing machine manufacturers will honour their guarantee if you don't follow their 'instructions for use'. In the same way, we are unable to accept liability for any loss arising from mistakes or misunderstandings on your part. So take time to read this book carefully.

Although this book points you in the right direction, reading one small book will not make you an expert, and there are times when you may need to take advice from professionals. This book is not a definitive statement of the law, although we believe it to be accurate as at September 2003.

The authors and publisher cannot accept liability for any advice or material that becomes obsolete due to subsequent changes in the law after publication, although every effort will be made to show any changes in the law that take place after the publication date on the companion website.

About the authors

Rosy Border, co-author of this title and series editor of the *Pocket Lawyer* series, has a first class honours degree in French and has worked in publishing, lecturing, journalism and the law. A prolific author and adapter, she stopped counting after 150 titles.

Jane Moir has a degree in law and politics and qualified as a solicitor over 15 years ago. She has practised extensively in family law, and is a member of both the Solicitors Family Law Association and the Law Society's Family Law Panel. As a qualified mediator, she believes in keeping divorce as amicable as possible and in 'divorce with dignity'.

Acknowledgments

A glance at the 'Useful contacts' will show the many sources we dipped into while writing this book. Thank you, everybody, especially Frances Burton of Lincoln's Inn Fields, London, who read this book and gave it her blessing, and John Rabson, Chartered Engineer, for IT support and refreshments.

Welcome

Welcome to *Pocket Lawyer*. Let's face it, the law is a maze and you are likely to get lost unless you have a map. This book is your map through the part of the maze that deals with family law.

We put *you* in control

This book empowers you. This is a good thing but being in control means responsibility as well as power, so please use this book properly. Read it with care and don't be afraid to make notes – we have left wide margins for you to do just that. Take your time – do not skip anything:

○ everything is there for a purpose;

○ if anything were unimportant, we would have left it out.

Think of yourself as a driver using a road map. The map tells you the route, but it is up to you to drive carefully along it.

Sometimes you are in danger of getting out of your depth and you will need to take professional advice. Watch out for the hazard sign.

Sometimes we pause to explain something: the origin of a word, perhaps, or why a particular piece of legislation was passed. You do not need to know these things to make use of this book, but we hope you find them interesting.

Sometimes we stop to empower you to do something. Look out for the 'Power points' sign.

Clear English rules OK

Client to solicitor who has just drafted a contract for him: 'This *can't* be legal – I can understand it!'

Our style is WYSIWYG – what you see is what you get.

Some legal documents have traditionally been written in archaic language, often known as 'law-speak'. This term also extends to the practice of using the names of legal cases as shorthand for legal concepts. This wording has stood the test of time – often several centuries – and has been hallowed by the courts. Some of the words used sound just like everyday language, but beware – it is a kind of specialist shorthand. When we *do* need to use technical language, we offer clear explanations: see 'Buzzwords', p xiii. These words appear in the text in **bold** so you can check their meaning.

A note on sex

This book is unisex. We acknowledge that there are both male and female members of every group and we try to allow for that in the text by using, wherever possible, the generic *they/them* rather than *he/she*, *him/her*, etc. Meanwhile, with great reluctance, we decided to use *spouse* rather than *husband or wife* (cumbersome) or *partner* (partners are not necessarily married).

A note on Scotland and Northern Ireland

This book is not wholly reliable for jurisdictions other than England and Wales.

Click onto the website

www.cavendishpublishing.com/pocketlawyer

A note on Petitioners and Respondents

There are two sides to everything, and in every **divorce** there has to be:

o a **Petitioner** (see 'Buzzwords', p xix) asking the court for a divorce; and

o a **Respondent** (see 'Buzzwords', p xix) responding – replying to the Petitioner's request.

In divorce proceedings the Petitioner makes most of the running, particularly where the paperwork is concerned, so in that section of the book we devote more space to the Petitioner's side of things.

We know of several couples who, after deciding a divorce was inevitable, chose which of them should be the Petitioner and which the Respondent. Choices might be based on something as basic as form-filling skills.

Almost all of this book applies equally to both **parties** (see 'Buzzwords', p xviii) and we devote a chapter to the Respondent's role in the proceedings.

What this book can do for you

This book contains:

o **conciliation**, separation or **divorce**? – exploring your options;

o separation questionnaire – to help you to decide what to put in a Separation Agreement;

o a sample Separation Agreement with clauses to suit individual cases;

o the paperwork that both the **Petitioner** and the **Respondent** need for a simple, uncontested divorce;

o the paperwork you need to make arrangements for the children – by mutual agreement;

o the advice you need to make financial arrangements – by mutual agreement;

o advice on obtaining **Legal Help** (see 'Buzzwords', p xvii), which is a form of **public funding**;

o   emergencies – chiefly domestic violence. In a real emergency, you cannot expect peaceful negotiation. We advise you on getting protection for yourself and any children – fast – and the possibility of negotiating later.

Additionally, this book gives you:

o   the general information that professional advisers would give you on the subject, if only they had the time to do so, and if only you had the money to pay them;

o   the 'buzzwords' that are important in this section of the law, and what they mean;

o   the answers to some of the most frequently asked questions (FAQs) on the subject;

o   access to a regularly updated companion website (www.cavendishpublishing.com/pocketlawyer).

What this book can't do for you

It can't make your decisions for you.

We realise that you and your spouse will not be on the best of terms. We don't expect you to sit on the sofa and read this book together. All the same, it will take co-operation to make this book work. This is because *the two of you must agree* whether to divorce, and if so:

o   what type of divorce to apply for (we list these on p 68);

o   what arrangements should be made for the children;

o   who is to live where;

o   what financial arrangements are to apply.

This book *does not* provide the tools for:

o   a contested divorce;

o   disputes over children;

o   disputes over money.

If you envisage anything of that sort you will need a solicitor and – given that solicitors charge by the hour – possibly quite a lot of money, depending on how protracted the dispute is.

Buzzwords

Here are some terms you will come across in this book. Please do not skip this section, as many of the terms used by lawyers have special meanings. Here we make them clear. The terms appear in **bold** in the text.

Acknowledgment of Service – the form the court sends to the **Respondent** (see below) with the **divorce petition**. The Respondent signs the Acknowledgment of Service and sends it back to the court to confirm that they have received the divorce petition.

affidavit – written evidence which replaces spoken evidence in court. Believers *swear* on the Bible, Q'ran, etc; people with no religious beliefs *affirm*. You will need to swear or affirm an affidavit as evidence that the facts in your **divorce petition** are true.

ancillary relief – the term that lawyers use for the money and property side of divorce. 'Ancillary' means 'secondary, a side issue'; the financial side is secondary to the break-up itself.

annulment (also known as **nullity**) – the cancelling of a marriage as if it had never happened. Annulling a marriage is exceptional but would apply, for example, in cases of bigamy.

answer – an official reply to a **divorce petition**, usually defending yourself against what you see as false accusations of unreasonable **behaviour** ('You stormed out in a huff.' 'Oh no I didn't!' 'Oh yes you did!').

Applicant – the person petitioning for a **divorce** is called the **Petitioner**. The person who is applying to the court for anything else, such as an **injunction**, an order concerning the children of the family, or **ancillary relief**, is called the Applicant. The Petitioner can therefore also be referred to as the Applicant if they have made an application for something else as well as asking for a divorce. The other side is still called the **Respondent**.

Application for Directions for Trial – a formal request to the court saying that you want the case to go ahead.

'**behaviour**' – one of the 'reasons' for **divorce**. The wording on the divorce **petition** says, 'The **Respondent** has behaved in such a way that the **Petitioner** cannot reasonably be expected to live with the Respondent'.

Certificate of Entitlement to a Decree – a paper signed by a judge, saying that you have proved your point and setting a date for the **Decree Nisi** to be pronounced.

Child Support Agency (CSA) – a government body set up to calculate, collect and enforce payment of child maintenance payments by what used to be called the 'absent parent' – that is, the parent who does not live with the child. In this book we sometimes talk about a '**non-resident parent**', in the sense of a parent who does not live with the child(ren) (see also **parent with care**, below).

clean break – a court order (usually a **Consent Order**) which enables the two individuals to walk away from the marriage without either having any further financial claim on the other. *Note*: a true clean break is *not* possible if there are dependent children.

client care letter – the standard letter solicitors send to each client explaining the terms under which they work, the hourly rate chargeable, who will handle the case and whom to approach in case of complaint.

conciliation – sessions with an impartial third person to help couples to:

ɔ   come to terms with the breakdown of their marriage;

ɔ   reach an agreement (or reduce disagreement) in matters such as children, the **matrimonial** home, finance, etc;

ɔ   sort out arrangements for the future.

(See also **mediation**.)

Consent Order – a court order in which both parties agree the financial arrangements (often, but not necessarily, a **clean break**) and the judge rubber-stamps them to make them legally binding. *Consent* in this context means 'agreement'.

contact – 'visiting rights' for **non-resident parents** and their children.

Contact Order – an order from a court which requires the parent with whom the children live to allow the child to visit, be visited by or stay with the **non-resident parent**.

Co-respondent – the other man or woman involved in an adultery **suit**: the third side of the eternal triangle.

county court – the court which deals with **divorce petitions**. Cases are *heard* (law-speak for 'considered') by judges (see also **Family Proceedings Court**).

cross-petition – a sort of tit-for-tat **divorce petition**, where the **Petitioner** has **filed** a divorce petition against the **Respondent**, who then files a petition of their own against the Petitioner. Not surprisingly, the **Legal Services Commission** does not fund cross-petitions and we don't recommend them.

decree – an order from the court. Judges can issue or pronounce decrees.

Decree Absolute – the certificate that makes the **divorce** final and irreversible (except by remarrying your ex as Elizabeth Taylor and Richard Burton did!).

Decree Nisi – a certificate that says you may have your **divorce** when you have served your time, which is six weeks and a day after the Decree Nisi date. On (or after) that day the **Petitioner** can apply for the **Decree Absolute**, which finalises the divorce.

defended divorce – **divorce** proceedings in which one **spouse files** a divorce **petition** but the other refuses to accept that the marriage is over and wants to stay married. This is different from **cross-petitioning** (see above), where both **parties** accept that the marriage is over, but disagree about whose fault it is!

directions – instructions from the court. A judge may arrange a directions **hearing**, for example, in disputes about children. During the hearing the judge will issue directions saying what is to happen next.

disbursements – expenses; the money solicitors have to pay out on your behalf. A typical disbursement would be a court fee.

Disbursements is law-speak for 'expenses: money paid out'. It comes from old French '*bourse*', a purse. Also, of course, a bursar keeps a tight hold on the purse strings and a bursary is an award of money.

---

divorce – the formal ending of a marriage, making a couple into two individuals.

ex parte – without the other side in a dispute being there. In family law, judges may issue an **injunction** (see below) *ex parte* to protect one **spouse** from domestic violence at the hands of the other. There is then a sort of return match *inter partes* (with both sides present) a week or so later, when the other **party** attends court to tell their side of the story (see Chapter 8).

Lord Woolf is trying manfully to banish Latin and medieval French from the courts, but nobody has yet found a snappy translation for *ex parte* and *inter partes*. 'Without notice/with notice' doesn't quite convey the same meaning.

Family Proceedings Court – the magistrates' court where cases are heard by magistrates (usually, but not always, non-lawyers with a qualified lawyer as clerk to the court).

file (with) – pass or send to the court (first-class post or delivery by hand is fine).

ground(s) for divorce – a valid reason for granting a **divorce** on the basis that the marriage has broken down irretrievably.

hearing – judges *hear* cases (before giving a judgment) and a hearing is an occasion when a judge does this.

hearing date – the day when your case goes to court. This may also be referred to as the 'return date'.

injunction – an order by a court for someone to do, or refrain from doing, something. In cases of domestic violence, the victim might apply for an injunction to restrain a violent **spouse** (see Chapter 8).

judicial separation – **divorce** in all but name. A **decree** of judicial separation does not end the marriage but removes the couple's duty to live together.

jurisdiction – the extent of a court's power and/or the territory in which a legal system applies. This book deals with the law in England and Wales.

Legal Help Scheme – free legal advice and assistance under the **Legal Services Commission's** scheme (formerly called the 'Green Form Scheme').

Just as road signs still show a steam locomotive, lawyers still talk about green forms because the form used to be pale green. The new form is white and is known as a 'Legal Help Form'.

Legal Services Commission – formerly the Legal Aid Board: the body which provides **public funding** (formerly called Legal Aid) for people who meet certain strict financial criteria.

litigant in person – a litigant is someone taking legal action, and a litigant in person is someone representing themselves in court, as opposed to instructing a lawyer. In straightforward DIY **divorce** proceedings the two **parties** are litigants in person, but there is no need for them to attend court.

lump sum order – a court order for one **spouse** to pay the other a set sum, all in one chunk (often in lieu of continuing maintenance).

maintenance pending suit – money to keep one **spouse** going until they get their **divorce** and/or the details of their **ancillary relief** are finalised.

matrimonial – to do with marriage. Lawyers often say *matrimonial* when most other people would say *family*. Wherever possible (though see **matrimonial home rights**) we prefer *family*, for example, *the family home*.

matrimonial home rights (previously known as *rights of occupation*) – your right to remain in the family home even if it is in your **spouse's** sole name.

mediation – help from an impartial third person (a **mediator**) to help couples considering separation or **divorce** to communicate better, to reduce conflict between them and to reach their own mutually agreed decisions about children, finances, property, etc. Mediation is not an attempt to salvage a marriage, although that may sometimes happen, but rather a sort of damage limitation exercise to help couples to end their relationship amicably.

non-molestation order – an order from the court (see also **injunction**) not to assault, harass or otherwise pester someone.

non-resident parent – formerly known as *absent parent* – the **Child Support Agency's** phrase for a parent who does not live with a child who is on their books (the parent the child lives with is called the **parent with care**).

notice – in this context, warning that a court **hearing** will take place. A hearing without notice is often referred to as *ex parte*.

Notice of Issue of Petition and Postal Service – a paper from the court saying that they have issued a **divorce petition** and **served** it on the **Respondent** by post, and giving the case a reference number.

occupation order – an order from a court either for **spouse** A to leave the family home or for spouse B to be allowed to move in again (see p 51).

parent with care (of a child) – the **Child Support Agency's** phrase for the parent with whom a child lives (as opposed to the **non-resident parent**).

parental responsibility – a catch-all phrase relating to the duties, powers and rights of a parent in relation to a child.

party – law-speak for a person involved in a court case.

periodic payments – weekly or monthly (maintenance) payments.

petition – an application for a **divorce**; **petitioning** is applying for a divorce and the **Petitioner** is the **spouse** asking for a divorce.

prayer – a request to the court to grant a **divorce** and any other associated things (for example, costs, **periodic payments**, lump sums, **Property Adjustment Orders**, etc).

privileged – confidential. Anything said or written that is 'privileged' may only be reported to the court if everyone involved in the discussions or correspondence agrees to this.

Prohibited Steps Order – an order of the court to prevent something from happening without the court's consent, such as taking a child out of the country.

Property Adjustment Order – a court order saying who is to have what property, for example, the family home.

public funding (formerly Legal Aid) – means-tested legal assistance from the **Legal Services Commission**.

Residence Order – an order from the court about where a child is to live and with whom. *Residence* has replaced *custody*, with its implications of 'remanded in ...'.

Respondent – the other **party**: the counterpart to the **Petitioner** (see above). A handy memory aid is 'the Petitioner applies and the Respondent replies'.

secured periodic payments – payments which are secured in some way, such as by a charge (like a mortgage) on the payer's house.

serve (on) – to send or hand a document to the other **party** in a case and be able to prove that you have done so. For example, the court *serves* the **divorce petition** on the **Respondent** and sends the **Petitioner** a certificate of service to confirm this.

Courts and lawyers *serve* documents on people to whom ordinary mortals post, fax or deliver by hand.

Specific Issue Order – an order of the court about a particular question that has arisen in relation to a child, and on which the parents disagree. This may concern religion, health, etc.

spouse – the unisex word for husband or wife. All spouses are married; partners need not be.

Statement of Arrangements for Children – the form enclosed with a **divorce petition**, which sets out the arrangements for the children: where they will live and with whom, and what **contact** they will have with the **non-resident parent**.

statutory charge – money the **Legal Services Commission** claws back to pay its fees (see p 58 for a full explanation).

suit – a fancy name for a law case (out of the same stable as 'sue').

swear – say on oath, in the presence of a solicitor or an officer of the court, that a statement is true (see **affidavit**, above). Non-believers can affirm instead.

undertaking – a solemn promise to the court. Breaking an undertaking is a serious matter and could result in imprisonment.

'Cross my heart and hope to die; Strike me dead if I tell a lie'. An oath was originally intended to frighten the witness into telling the truth through the threat of supernatural vengeance. English common law maintained that non-believers would not feel bound by an oath because they did not believe in a deity who would punish them if they lied. Nowadays, non-believers are allowed to give evidence; they affirm instead of swearing.

Frequently asked questions (FAQs)

I have been married just six months and it has been a disaster. How soon can I get a divorce?

You cannot obtain a **divorce** until you have been married for one year. In some circumstances you might be able to apply for **judicial separation** or **annulment** before the 12 months are up, but neither is a DIY matter and neither is instant. You would need to explain your particular circumstances to a solicitor to see if there was anything to be gained by going down that route. You can, of course, simply separate now, and if you are really miserable together this may be the wisest course of action.

I would like some general advice on divorce. I recall my sister getting an interview for a fixed £5 fee. Does this still apply?

No. The scheme was abolished in 1993 and has not been replaced. However, many solicitors offer fixed-fee interviews, though the fee is usually considerably more than £5. Some offer 15 minutes or even half an hour free of charge. A session like this is often called a 'diagnostic interview'. Look in your local *Yellow Pages* under 'Solicitors', compile a hit list and ask the receptionist of each firm whether they offer this service.

My friend's marriage break-up cost a fortune in legal fees. Can I get a divorce without using a solicitor?

Yes – *provided everything is straightforward and non-contentious*. We show you how to do this for just the court fees, which at the time of writing are £210 (£180 to issue proceedings and £30 to make the **decree** absolute). Most court staff are helpful and will glance over your paperwork to make sure nothing is missing. However, **divorce** itself is only part of the story. It is likely that the bulk of your friend's legal costs involved the financial side of the break-up or problems over the arrangements for children. This is why it is better to try to agree rough, ballpark financial arrangements before you consult solicitors, who can then fine-tune them and get them 'blessed' by the court.

I want a divorce, but I can't find our marriage certificate. What can I do?

Send for a copy from the Registrar of Births, Deaths and Marriages for the place where you were married, which will cost you £6.50 and will take about two weeks. If you want it urgently, they can get a copy out to you by the next working day for £22. You must state:

o   full name of groom;

o   full name of bride (maiden surname);

o   date and place of ceremony.

A second option is to apply to the central General Register Office (see 'Useful contacts' for details). There is an application form – PAS8M. It will cost you £11.50, or £27.50 if you wish them to send it to you within two working days, in which case mark the envelope 'Priority'.

If you were married abroad and the marriage certificate is not in English, you will have to get it translated. If the translation is done abroad it will have to be *notarised*, that is, **sworn** to be accurate. Translations done in the UK are usually backed up by an **affidavit** to the same effect. Look up 'Translators' in the *Yellow Pages*.

My wife is applying for a divorce. Will I have to go to court?

Not for a straightforward **divorce**. The judge will go through the paperwork and will, if all is correct, grant her a **Decree Nisi**. Disputes over money, children, etc, later are a different matter: couples who cannot agree such things may end up asking a judge to decide, which could involve appearing in court.

My home is in the UK and I got married here, but I spend a lot of time working abroad. Can I get a divorce in the UK?

Almost certainly. Turn to p 73 where we quote: 'The Court has jurisdiction under Article 2(1) of the Council Regulation on the following grounds ...' and then we explain about residence and domicile. If one of these grounds fits your case, you are in the clear. If in doubt, seek professional advice.

I have married someone who I now know was married already. Can I get a divorce?

You don't *need* a **divorce**, because your marriage is 'void' – invalid; you have never been legally married. Technically speaking, you were never married at all. However, it is wise to get a court order for the **annulment** of the 'marriage', as you can then apply to the court for **ancillary relief**; also, your status will then be clear if you ever wish to marry 'properly'.

Annulment is not a DIY procedure. Seek legal advice.

I have heard about 'quickie divorces'. (a) Can I get one? (b) How quick are they?

(a)   Yes, possibly – see below.

(b)   How long is a piece of string?

'Quickie' in this context just means 'undefended'. All **divorces** under the current legislation are 'quickie divorces' unless the **Respondent** defends.

A 'no-fault' divorce by mutual consent, where neither **party** blames the other, would require two years' separation. To obtain a divorce in under two years, one of you would have to say that the other was guilty either of adultery or of **behaviour**. In both instances, therefore, one of you will have to blame the other, with all the accompanying hurt and anger that this might bring.

After that, it will depend on how busy your local court is, how prompt each party is in turning the paperwork around and how speedily you can finalise your financial and other arrangements. There is, in any case, a built-in waiting period of six weeks between the **Petitioner** being granted a **Decree Nisi** and being allowed to apply for the **decree** to be made absolute. Three to four months, with everything going smoothly, would be an absolute minimum.

Do I need to name the Co-respondent in my adultery petition?

No, you need not name them (see p 82). Naming the **Co-respondent** in an adultery **petition** can be a spiteful thing to do, because **divorce** papers are **served** on the Co-respondent as well as on the **Respondent**. Quite apart from whether being spiteful is good for your soul, you might well spare your children, and the Co-respondent's family too, a lot of unhappiness, save on legal fees and even get a better financial settlement if you can keep the emotional temperature down.

Naming the Co-respondent can also cause practical problems and delay your divorce. For example, naming the Co-respondent means they also have to be served with a copy of the petition. If the Co-respondent fails, or refuses, to return an **Acknowledgment of Service** form, then *you* are left with the problem of serving it on them personally, or arranging for service by a court bailiff. Sometimes your **spouse** may not have given you the correct spelling of the Co-respondent's surname or their correct address. Both of these must be correct or substantial delay will result. If in doubt, leave it out!

We have agreed between ourselves where the children are to live, and arranged 'visiting rights'. Do we need to go to court to confirm this?

No. Whoever of you is the **Petitioner** will **file** a **Statement of Arrangements for Children** with the **divorce petition**, and the judge will take this into account when deciding whether to grant a divorce. The law normally takes the view that there should only be court orders in respect of children if the parents cannot agree or if an agreement later breaks down. Unless you have proposed something outrageous or missed out something vital (it happens!), the Statement of Arrangements should be 'blessed' by the judge without anyone having to go to court. The court will then state that it is satisfied with the arrangements.

Is there any way I can make my husband pay maintenance for me and our child before our divorce is finalised?

Yes. You can apply to the court for **maintenance pending suit** – for which you will need professional advice. It is better and cheaper, of course, to agree something between you. Sit down with the figures and sort it out.

I am on income support and cannot afford the court fees. Will this stop me getting a divorce?

No. There is a special form (EX160) to apply for remission of court fees. You can see a sample form on the Court Service website (www.courtservice.gov.uk).

Moreover, if you are receiving income support (or one of several other kinds of state benefit), you will almost certainly qualify for free professional advice and assistance too, whether you are the **Petitioner** or the **Respondent**. Choose a solicitor who holds a **Legal Services Commission** (LSC) franchise; you should not have to pay anything at all because the LSC pays your fees for you (see Chapter 10).

I shall be on income support after my divorce and my husband has not yet told me how much maintenance he will be paying for our children. Who can advise?

The **Child Support Agency (CSA)** will automatically become involved, because you are receiving state benefits. The CSA will assess your ex's income and outgoings and set a figure for maintenance payments. Your own welfare benefits will be adjusted accordingly. Some people say the CSA should be renamed the Treasury Support Agency because that's where some of your ex's maintenance payments will go! (See p 21 for more details.)

Our family home is in my husband's sole name and he is threatening to kick me out. Can he do this?

No. You have 'rights of occupation' (or **matrimonial home rights**) until the fate of the property is decided (that is, after your **divorce** proceedings) and provided you stay put, your husband cannot evict you without a court order. Moreover, you can prevent your husband from selling the home without your knowledge (see Chapter 17).

My wife and I have lived apart for many years without any problems, but I would now like to remarry. My wife, however, does not want a divorce. What can I do?

If you have been separated for at least five years, you can get a **divorce** without your wife's agreement (see p 67).

My wife has gone to live with the local vicar, a lady named Sarah. Can I divorce my wife for adultery?

Adultery is usually understood to be committed with someone of the opposite sex. Rather than baffle the judge, you should use **behaviour** (see p 68).

Can we work it out?

A troubled marriage

Marriages can get into trouble for a variety of reasons. Sometimes you can grit your teeth and soldier on in the hope that you are just going through a bad patch and that things will get better. Often they do; every marriage has peaks, troughs and plateaux.

Sharing your troubles with friends who have survived similar experiences can be helpful, but you may reach the point where you need to explore other options:

o **conciliation** and counselling;

o separation; or

o **divorce**.

You need to be aware of the implications of your choice on:

o your children;

o your finances;

o your home.

We explore the options with you but first of all, remember – and we print it in huge letters:

IT NEEDN'T BE ANYBODY'S FAULT!

There is far less talk about guilty and innocent **parties** than there used to be. In ordinary divorce proceedings the courts are not in the retribution business. They are not interested in punishing anybody for bad behaviour or rewarding anyone for virtue. If, after examining all the options, you do decide to seek a divorce, you will find that the courts are far more interested in protecting the vulnerable – especially children – than in blaming either **spouse** for the break-up of the marriage. For the sake of those same children, not to mention your family and friends, it is important to settle everything as calmly as possible.

Talking it over

If you and your **spouse** are still on speaking terms, it may be worth trying to resolve your differences yourselves. Meeting on neutral ground, with a written agenda like a business meeting, is one strategy which some couples find helpful, but this takes a lot of goodwill on both sides, and without a third person to referee the discussion there is a danger that the more forceful personality will have all their own way.

If you find it difficult to talk out your problems without one or other of you getting bulldozed, or the discussion degenerating into a screaming match, you should consider calling in a **mediator**.

Couples in trouble have a wide choice of skilled help to assist them in making sense of their problems – money, the family home, business issues, debts and, not least, the children – and to steer them towards a solution without incurring crippling legal costs.

In 1996 a new Act was passed. At the time of writing, the parts of the Family Law Act 1996 relating to divorce have not come into force (Part IV relating to domestic violence is, however, in force) and the Department for Constitutional Affairs has announced that it will not be brought into force in its present form. The aim of this Act is to discourage couples from starting **divorce** proceedings before they have tried **mediation**. Even though the Act has not become law, it is already influencing the thinking both of professionals and of the **Legal Services Commission** (**LSC**). The LSC requires couples to attend a mediation screening appointment before their solicitors can apply on their behalf for a full **public funding** certificate. You do not, however, have to attend a mediation screening appointment to obtain legal advice under the **Legal Help Scheme** (for more details about the Legal Help Scheme and public funding, see p 55).

Conciliation and counselling

Forget words like *conciliatory*, with undertones of appeasement, placation and sucking-up. **Conciliation** in this context simply means getting a third person, usually a trained counsellor, to help you both to resolve your problems for yourselves.

The difficulty with conciliation or marriage guidance counselling is that it takes time to set it up, and you may need (or believe you need) help at once. There may, according to local needs and conditions, be a waiting list of several months to see a Relate counsellor (see 'Useful contacts', p 168, for details). We know couples who, by the time their appointment with Relate came up, had decided to give their marriage another chance.

You may face a long or inconvenient trip to your nearest counsellor. Provision is not uniform – much depends on where you live, and the nearest counsellor may be many miles away with only minimal public transport available. Couples without a car are really penalised here.

Even so, conciliation is always worth considering and worth any amount of inconvenience if it works for you. Clearly, if your **spouse** has just come home roaring drunk and knocked you about (and if they have, you should turn to Chapter 8 *now!*), an appointment with a counsellor in three weeks' time is not much help. However, in general it is unwise to decide that your relationship is damaged beyond repair without giving conciliation a chance.

Possibilities are as follows:

o   Relate (see 'Useful contacts' and your local telephone directory);

o   local organisations (such as, in Suffolk, PACT (Parents' Conciliation Trust)) that specialise in looking after the needs of the children (check with your local Citizens Advice Bureau (CAB) for details of similar organisations in your area);

o   some doctors' surgeries which can refer patients to independent counsellors – ask your doctor what is available locally; or

○   look on notice boards in your public library, call the CAB to find out what is available locally, and check out 'Useful contacts'.

Mediation

Many couples agree to call in a third person, called a **mediator**, to help them to resolve areas of disagreement or dispute. There are big advantages over slugging it out between solicitors – not least the saving in cost – even though many mediators nowadays are qualified solicitors who have taken a special course.

Mediators are impartial. They have no authority to make any decisions about your dispute(s). A mediator will help you to reach a decision for yourselves, resolving your disagreements by negotiation.

Mediation is not the same as counselling

Counselling is about feelings and a **mediator** may suggest that you see a counsellor if they think you need help in understanding and handling your feelings. *Counselling is intended to help couples to stay together.*

Mediation accepts that some relationships do break down, and if yours is one of these, the mediator will help you to sort out your practical and legal arrangements for the future.

Mediation can be used at any stage, whether you are trying to stay together or whether you are in the final stages of **divorce**. We are mentioning it here only because you need to be aware of it. You might decide to try it at a much later stage – for example, to resolve a dispute over financial matters – and that would be quite in order.

Mediation sessions are private and quite informal. You will normally need between two and four sessions of about 90 minutes each.

Mediation can help you to sort out:

○   arrangements for your children;

○   dividing up your property;

○   financial details;

and any other practical issues associated with your separation or divorce.

If mediation is being used to discuss arrangements for your children, the mediator will expect you to consider the children's needs and wishes first.

If mediation is being used to deal with property or financial arrangements, the mediator will ask you both to fill in a form giving full details of your property, loans, debts, income, outgoings and any other relevant information. This form is available at www.courtservice.gov.uk/cms/media/forme.pdf. You will probably find it helpful in sorting out your finances, whether or not you decide to go for mediation.

This factual information may be used later in court to help with any financial arrangements; it is, however, the only information that will be passed on. Anything that either of you says during the sessions is **privileged** and the mediator will not divulge it unless you both give your permission, with one important exception – *if the mediator considers that any child or adult has suffered significant harm or is at risk of being harmed, then the mediator will inform the police or social services.*

All mediators are specially qualified. As we said above, many are solicitors who have also taken a further course in mediation. Others are members of the UK College of Family Mediators or the Family Mediators' Association (see 'Useful contacts', p 168).

There is no fixed fee for mediation: different mediators charge different rates. If you are on a low income, you may not have to pay anything.

Mediators have a duty to ensure that all sessions are conducted fairly and that both **parties** feel safe. Mediators are impartial. They are not adjudicators and they are not advocates either – they do not judge and they do not take sides.

We repeat: mediators have no authority to make any decisions regarding your disputes. Their job is to help you to resolve your disagreements yourselves, by negotiation.

When is mediation *not* the answer?

○ When someone is less than frank and honest.

For mediation to work successfully, both **spouses** must be frank with each other.

○ When someone feels unsafe or intimidated.

Neither spouse should feel threatened or pressurised by the other.

○ When the dispute is something you cannot be expected to resolve for yourselves.

For these reasons, **mediation** is *not* the answer:

○ if either of you lacks the mental capacity to take part in mediation;

○ where there is violent **behaviour** on the part of one (or both) of you;

○ where emergency proceedings have to be taken, such as child protection issues or violence within the family;

○ where there is a court order banning one spouse from having contact with the other;

○ in financial disputes where either of you is bankrupt;

○ in certain matters where only the court can decide, such as in cases involving the paternity of a child;

○ where marital therapy or counselling would be more helpful.

On the other hand, there is a lot to be said for mediation:

○ it helps you to find a solution which both spouses feel is fair. There will not be any winner or loser. Instead, mediation is intended to help you to reach sensible, practical arrangements;

○ it can help to reduce animosity and misunderstandings between the two spouses;

○ it improves communication between spouses, which is particularly important if you have children.

Is separation an option for you?

Reasons for separating

Suppose you and your **spouse** have decided you can no longer bear to live together. Here are some possible reasons for finding life as a couple intolerable:

o you are miserable together;

o you want time out in the hope of saving your marriage;

o someone is at risk if you stay together (if this is you, turn at once to Chapter 8);

o you have decided that you may want a **divorce** on the grounds of separation (see below) rather than for one of the other reasons, or, as the court calls them, 'facts'.

'Facts' for divorce

To qualify for a **divorce**, you must show that the marriage has *broken down irretrievably*. The court recognises five 'facts' for this irretrievable breakdown. Before we consider your options further, let's look at these 'facts' for a court to grant a divorce, because they will influence any decision you may make about separation. Here are all five, although in practice the fifth seldom arises nowadays.

1 Your **spouse** has committed adultery and you find it unbearable to continue living with them.

2   Your spouse has behaved in such a way, and to such an extent, that you find it unbearable to continue living with them, and objectively it is not 'reasonable' for you to continue to do so. The wording on the divorce **petition** says, 'The **Respondent** has behaved in such a way that the **Petitioner** cannot reasonably be expected to live with the Respondent'.

There are no hard and fast rules here, but the key word is 'reasonable'. Your spouse's behaviour could be very bad indeed (such as chronic drunkenness and/or violence), but it need not be so, provided that it is not 'reasonable' for you to put up with it. You can see some examples of '**behaviour**', ranging from mildly unreasonable to atrocious, in Chapter 20.

3   You and your spouse have lived apart for two years and you both agree to a divorce.

4   You and your spouse have lived apart for five years – one of you can obtain a divorce without the other's agreement.

5   Your spouse has deserted you.

Facts 1 and 2 would enable you to apply for a divorce without a period of separation, so long as you have been married for at least one year. The tabloid newspapers sometimes refer to such divorces as 'quickie divorces' because wronged spouses can **file** a petition immediately, without a compulsory separation period. In practice, they are not very quick – three to four months is about the quickest you can expect – but they are at least quicker than two years' separation.

If one of you is in a hurry to marry someone else, 1 or 2 would be the facts to consider, provided you did not mind blaming the marriage breakdown on your spouse and provided they did not mind being blamed. We'll come back to these in more detail later.

To qualify for fact 3 or 4, you would need to live apart for the qualifying period, so you would separate and mark the date of separation in your respective diaries.

A note on judicial separation

We have heard couples say, 'We're having a judicial separation'. Most are mistaken. A **judicial separation** isn't just any old separation. It is a separation which has been 'blessed' by a court and made official.

Some cultures and religions frown on **divorce**, even in the face of adultery or cruelty. In those circumstances, couples separate permanently in preference to obtaining a divorce. A **decree** of judicial separation does not require the agreement of the other **spouse**. The procedure is the same as for a divorce (see flowchart, pp 64–66), but without the final split.

Judicial separation for other reasons is not common. There are a few cases, however, when obtaining a decree of judicial separation, as opposed to a divorce, is a wise or prudent thing to do. For example, couples who are near to retirement or already retired may wish to keep their pension rights intact (for example, widow's pension). A **Decree Absolute** in divorce ends these rights, while a decree of judicial separation does not. In such cases, see a solicitor.

Under one roof?

Let us suppose that you decide to separate, either to give yourselves time out from a difficult relationship or as a basis for a **divorce** by mutual agreement in two years' time.

If your house is big enough, or if you can work out a rota to use the kitchen and bathroom, you could in theory live separate lives under one roof. In practice this can be quite difficult, but it does have three very big advantages:

o   it gives you time to sort out your financial affairs and arrangements concerning housing, including keeping any mortgage payments going;

o   there is less disruption for any children;

o   it is bound to be cheaper than maintaining separate households.

The downside of this arrangement is that it may be difficult to prove to a court that you have in fact lived separate lives under the same roof. You will need to convince the judge that:

o you have slept in separate bedrooms;

o you have cooked separate meals and eaten them apart;

o you have each done your own household chores;

o you have each done your own shopping;

o you have had your washing done separately;

o you have behaved like two strangers living under the same roof.

In a famous case, *Mouncer v Mouncer*, the judge refused to grant Mr and Mrs Mouncer a **divorce** because during their separation there had been a certain amount of family life – shared meals, etc – going on.

'Separate lives' means just that. It could be a fairly joyless existence, and you might even decide you would be happier living together after all.

Splitting up is rarely simple

Even without the complications of trying to live separate lives under one roof, many couples, after they have looked carefully at the implications of separating, decide to give their relationship another chance.

The legal process of breaking up is straightforward – *provided you are childless, homeless and penniless.* Such people can simply walk away from each other and stop living together. For anyone else, there are many things to consider. The more children, property and money you and your **spouse** have, the more you have to think about before you separate.

First, any children of the family have to be considered:

o Who will they live with?

o Who will support them?

o What contact will the other parent have with them?

Next there is the property and financial side:

o   What will happen to the family home?
o   What will each of you live on?
o   How will any assets be divided?
o   What about pension rights?

All these are problems which you must deal with, whether you are divorcing or only separating.

Apart – but still married

o   Separation is quick – in an emergency it can be instant.
o   You can separate without going to court.
o   Separation is reversible – you are still married and can get together again at any time.

Separation, however you go about it, keeps the marriage in existence even if your relationship has died. *You are still legally married.*

The upside of still being married is, of course, that you can get together again at any time. Meanwhile, you can use the time apart to think carefully about the future. If you decide to get together again, you can start afresh as if nothing had happened. That is a lot easier (not to mention cheaper) than emulating Elizabeth Taylor and Richard Burton and divorcing, only to remarry later.

Even if you are sure that no amount of time and space can change your mind, living apart for a while before you start **divorce** proceedings can help to reduce the bitterness and make the eventual divorce less painful for everyone.

It is probably fair to say that there is a period of separation – physical or emotional – before every divorce. We know of couples who (almost) enjoyed their separation. They would meet once a week to do the shopping together and would use this time to discuss any domestic details such as the children's school arrangements. The husband would come for supper once a week and afterwards do any small DIY chores around the house while his wife did his ironing. By the time they eventually **filed** for divorce they had sorted everything out amicably – and it did not cost them a penny in legal fees.

The downside of still being married is that *in the eyes of the law, you are still a couple.* So unless you change your will, your **spouse** will inherit your estate when you die. You will also need to think about the future of the family home. More about this on p 113.

Separation without agreement

This can mean:

o   one **spouse** walking out;

o   one spouse kicking the other out;

o   police and/or courts stepping in to remove one spouse for the protection of the other and/or the children.

These kinds of separation are drastic and can be instant. A court can order one spouse out of the family home. Orders are available in the magistrates' court and **county court** to protect vulnerable people from violence and harassment. If you need one of these, it is probably an emergency (turn to Chapter 8).

Separation with agreement

Suppose that your **spouse** is sensible and you believe the two of you can work something out and abide by it. You might decide to separate by agreement.

This may be:

o   an informal agreement; or

o   a formal agreement.

We explain both below. The distinction between an informal and a formal agreement is ours, and as such *has no force in law.*

Any agreement is pointless unless there is a good chance of both spouses sticking to it. Don't bother seeking an agreement of any kind if your spouse is:

o   violent;

o   a danger to you or to the children; or

o   thoroughly untrustworthy.

You may need a court order (see below) to make them behave.

Informal agreement

You have talked things over. You may also have exchanged letters, setting out what you have decided. There is no formal document, and you probably did not take legal advice, but you have worked out an arrangement and hope to stick to it.

For:

o   You sort everything out to suit your own needs.

o   It does not cost you any money.

o   Nobody else is involved. You did it your way.

Against:

o   You may regard your agreement as binding, but the court may not.

o   If either of you breaks a promise, it is hard to make them toe the line.

o   You might not get it right; the agreement might not do what you meant it to.

Formal written agreement

You have talked things over. You may also have exchanged letters setting out what you have decided. You then set out what you have agreed in a written agreement, probably based on the sample agreement at the back of this book, and you both sign and date it.

If you eventually **divorce**, you can use the financial and property aspects of your agreement as the basis for a legally binding **Consent Order** which will be 'blessed' by the court.

For:

o You sort everything out to suit your own needs.

o The cost is minimal.

o It is easier to enforce than an informal agreement.

o Courts will be more likely to accept it.

o Everything is properly set out: you know where you stand.

o If you decide on a divorce later, two years' separation will provide grounds, with no hard feelings.

o It isn't nearly as final as divorce!

Against:

o Courts can still overturn a Separation Agreement dealing with financial matters.

o The **Child Support Agency** can change child maintenance payments even if you are both happy with them.

o Neither of you will be able to **petition** for divorce for desertion (note, however, that very few people do anyway).

Ending a Separation Agreement

Typically, these events end a Separation Agreement:

o You **divorce**.

o Either of you dies.

o Both of you decide to end the agreement, for whatever reason.

o You get together again.

Agreeing to separate

What should a Separation Agreement cover?

Whether formal or informal, any Separation Agreement will need to cover the things you would have to work out if you were planning to divorce. These are, basically:

o   property;
o   money; and
o   children

– not necessarily in that order. We have printed a draft Separation Agreement in Chapter 6. Even if you decide to do things informally, it is worth using this as a sort of agenda of points to take into account.

Of course, every situation is unique and you may need to adapt our Agreement to suit your own circumstances. We show you how to go about this.

Here are some points to consider.

Dividing the assets

Separation seriously harms your wealth. Keeping up two households is bound to cost more than keeping up just one.

You will have to make a list of everything you own, individually and jointly, and decide who needs what.

o   Suppose you own the family home jointly, with a mortgage:

   – Who will live there?

   – Who will pay the mortgage?

- Will one of you buy the other out? (See also 'Housing', below.)

o What will happen to joint bank and building society accounts?

o What about pensions?

o Who will service any debts and/or hire purchase?

o Suppose you have a family car:

- Will you sell it and divide the proceeds?

- Or will the car go to the one who needs transport for work or the school run?

o What about furniture and other household items?

Consider, too, the consequences if one of you dies. Remember that if you die without making a will, by law your **spouse** will inherit all or a large chunk of your estate whether you are on good terms or not. Find out more about this in *Wills and Estate Planning* in the *Pocket Lawyer* series.

Housing

o Who will live where? Who will pay the rent or mortgage?

o Can one of you claim housing benefit (to help pay for rented accommodation) or income support (to help with mortgage payments)?

Maintenance

o for your **spouse**;

o for your children.

Even if you don't think you need any maintenance, or if your **spouse** is refusing to ask for any, put a nominal sum – even 5 p per year – in any Separation Agreement you make. Why bother? Because if your circumstances change, you can then go to court and get your maintenance allowance increased. If you don't put in any maintenance arrangements, you could find it hard to persuade a court to order any maintenance later on.

o Always allow for change – suppose one of you loses your job, retires, dies or even comes into a fortune?

o Remember that the **Child Support Agency** (see p 21) can in certain circumstances override any agreement regarding maintenance for children.

A word on benefits

We said earlier that marriage break-up damages your wealth. If you and your **spouse** separate or **divorce**, there may not be enough money to go round. You may need to consider claiming state benefits to help you manage financially, especially if your spouse is refusing to keep up payments you used to rely on before your separation.

'Useful contacts' directs you to a government website which lists state benefits you may never have known existed. Here, however, are some of the main ones. Remember that the estranged spouse of a rich person is classed as single and may thus qualify for benefits if they have little money of their own.

Job seeker's allowance is an option if you are able to work but are either not working or working on average less than 16 hours per week.

If you have children you may also be entitled to *child benefit*.

People are only entitled to *income support* if they are on a low income and have savings under a certain amount (usually £8,000 but not always), are over the age of 16 and are not working, or work on average less than 16 hours per week.

Anybody who is on a low income and paying rent can claim *housing benefit* and *Council Tax benefit*. If you have children and their other parent is living elsewhere, you may also claim *child support maintenance*. *Children's tax credit* is also a possibility for working parents.

You may qualify for an *emergency loan*, for example, for basic furnishings or removal costs if you move out of the family home.

If you apply for benefits, the DWP (Department for Work and Pensions, formerly the Department of Social Security (DSS)) will automatically send your spouse a **Child Support Agency** (**CSA**) form. They take the view that children should be supported by their parents rather than by the state.

Will you qualify for Legal Help?

The bad news: Breaking up, as we said before, should carry a wealth warning. Most vulnerable are wives with little or no money of their own.

The good news: A person who is separated from their **spouse** is considered as a single person, so even a rich man's wife, if she has little money of her own, may well qualify for **Legal Help**. Does this mean *you*? (See Chapter 10.)

Separation and children

You are talking about people, not possessions, here. It has always been self-evident that the children's needs must come first, and in the 1989 Children Act (see p 88) the law spelt this out: the word the Act uses is *paramount*. Our thesaurus suggests *chief, principal, supreme, dominant, central, overriding* ... you get the idea – children come first!

Keep the heat down!

Your children love you both and they will find it hard to understand why you don't seem to love each other any more. Any arrangements you make must disregard your own hurt feelings and concentrate on causing the children as little damage or upheaval as possible.

Some 'don'ts'

You may feel tempted to use a sympathetic child as a confidant. *Don't.*

Don't, under any circumstances, discuss the details of your marriage breakdown with your children. And *don't* try to persuade them that the break-up is all your **spouse's** fault *even if you are quite sure that it is true.*

Don't let young children see your bitterness towards your spouse. Children become very confused if one of their parents shows feelings of hatred or disgust for the other.

Don't let your children take sides.

Your children need to keep their love and respect for both parents, and this will become more and more important to them, and to you, as time goes on. In worst-case scenarios, where children are drawn into their parents' disputes they can be scarred emotionally, which can lead to behavioural problems. Their education is likely to suffer too, as any experienced teacher will tell you. To learn and develop and grow into happy, well-adjusted adults, children need a happy and secure environment.

It is probably very difficult for you to protect your children from the emotional warfare that is going on around them, especially if your spouse seems hellbent on breaking all the rules, but protect them you must. So keep the heat down!

We return to this subject on p 129 but make no apology for introducing it here.

Arrangements for children

Here are some typical questions to ask yourselves:

ɔ   Who will the children live with:

  –   during the week?

  –   at weekends?

ɔ   Maintenance – who will pay the bills?

ɔ   Contact:

  –   What arrangements will there be for the **non-resident parent** to see them?

  –   Can grandparents and other relations keep in touch too?

ɔ   Is there anything extra, such as school fees or hospital appointments, that may need to be dealt with in your case?

Even if you have no immediate plans for **divorce**, it is worth looking at the **Statement of Arrangements for Children** on p 139. This is a form which tells the court what arrangements will be made for the children when the couple split up, and it is very comprehensive. Use the questions in the form as guidelines for your discussions.

A word about the Child Support Agency (CSA)

Since April 1993, child maintenance has been the responsibility of the **Child Support Agency**, with the job of trying to get parents who do not live with their children (usually fathers, but not always) to maintain their children according to the CSA's assessment of their means.

The CSA provides a helpline and a website – see 'Useful contacts', p 166 – and has branches in main DWP (Department for Work and Pensions, formerly the DSS) offices.

The CSA has had a very bad press and an alarming percentage of its assessments seem to have been inaccurate, but its aim is a praiseworthy one: to shift responsibility for child maintenance from the state to the parent who has left home – why should parents be allowed to walk away from their responsibilities?

When does the CSA get involved?

o If the DWP is involved in the case, for example, if one parent is claiming income support.

o If you cannot agree the amount of maintenance and the **parent with care** asks the CSA for an assessment.

o If someone blows the whistle – for example, if a couple have had a child maintenance agreement which has broken down.

When does the CSA not get involved?

In general, if:

o no public money is involved;

o the parent with care is not receiving benefits, such as income support;

o the parent with care does not ask the CSA to intervene and nobody complains.

In general, if you are unable to agree about child maintenance the parent with care will ask the CSA to make an assessment.

The court has no power to intervene in cases where there is still a dispute about maintenance. However, it is possible for people involved in **divorce** or **judicial separation** proceedings to bypass the CSA by written agreement. It would not, however, be a DIY matter. You would need to seek professional advice.

The present arrangements

The CSA works out the amount of maintenance payable using a complex formula based on the income of the parent who is not living with the child(ren).

If you are the **parent with care** and:

o   you are not getting income support or job seeker's allowance; *and*

o   you cannot reach an agreement about maintenance with your **spouse**,

you can still use the CSA if the following apply to you:

o   there is no existing maintenance order concerning the child(ren);

o   the child(ren) is/are under 16 years of age, or if they are over 16 years but still in full-time secondary education;

o   your spouse is not living in the same household as the child(ren) *and* you live in the UK;

o   finally, perhaps most importantly, the child is the child by birth or adoption of *both yourself and your spouse*. Stepchildren cannot get support from their step-parents through the CSA.

The CSA can, unfortunately, take a very long time to process applications. Applications are meant to be processed by the CSA within 20 weeks, but it can take longer.

Child support legislation was recently changed by the Child Support Pensions and Social Security Act 2000, which came into force in April 2003.

Under the new provisions, the calculation for Child Support is much more straightforward. The CSA looks at the *net* income (see below) of the parent who does not live with the child(ren), and allocates:

15% for one child;
20% for two children;
25% for three or more children.

A person's net income is calculated by deducting tax and National Insurance and pension contributions from their total income.

If the *net* income of a parent not living with the children is low, then they will pay a reduced rate. If the **non-resident parent's** *net* income is more than £2,000 per week, then there is a cap on the amount of maintenance they have to pay, although the *parent with care* can apply to the CSA for increased payments by way of a top-up order.

As many parents were already subject to assessments by the CSA before April 2003, phasing-in provisions have been brought in to give them time to change pre-existing cases onto the new system. Phasing-in for such cases is expected to start in April 2004. Basically, any increase or decrease in the amount of child maintenance payable under the new provisions is capped to £10 per week each year.

Suppose, for example, that you were paying £80 per week under an existing child support assessment before April 2003, and suppose that the amount payable under the new law is £140 per week. In the first year from April 2004 you will have to pay £90 per week, then you will pay £100 per week in the second year and so on until you reach £140.

If the parent not living with the child(ren) has a new spouse or cohabitant with children of their own, or if the new relationship produces more children, then that will affect the amount of child maintenance payable for the non-resident parent's previous family. The CSA will assess this parent's *net* income, taking into account the needs of their new family as well as the family they left behind. So their *net* income is said to be 15% less if there is one child in the new family, 20% less if there are two children and 25% less if there are three or more children in the new family. These reductions are applied so that maintenance payable to the 'old' family is assessed on the reduced net income of the non-resident parent.

The parent not living with the child(ren) will also be able to ask the CSA to take the whole of any contributions they pay into a pension scheme into account as a valid deduction from their net income. Unfortunately, however, their housing costs will not be taken into account when calculating the amount of child support to be paid.

Maintenance payments also take account of the child(ren) staying overnight with the non-resident parent (the jargon is 'staying **contact**'). Maintenance is reduced by one-seventh for every night per week, taken as an average over a year, that each child spends with them. For example, if a child spends every Friday and Saturday night with the non-resident parent, this will reduce weekly child support payments to the parent with care by two-sevenths.

Under the new arrangements, a court order has a guaranteed shelf life of just 14 months. The **CSA** can now overturn court orders.

Suppose you are fortunate enough to agree maintenance between you and get the details included in a court order dealing with financial matters. If both parents are content, the order will continue. After a year has elapsed from the date of the order, however, either parent can, if they wish, opt out of the court order by giving two months' notice to the other parent. They can then apply to the CSA to set a level of maintenance. The CSA assessment will override the previous agreement and court order.

Full details are available either from the CSA or from your local DWP office.

5

Your separation questionnaire

This questionnaire will help you to draft your Separation Agreement. Some of the information will also be needed if you later decide to apply for a **divorce**.

First, the easy bits.

Your name

Your spouse's name

The address where *you* will be living.

The address where *your spouse* will be living.

Children: names and dates of birth

1 .... DOB ....

2 .... DOB ....

3 .... DOB ....

4 .... DOB ....

5 .... DOB ....

6 .... DOB ....

(Include any stepchildren, etc.)

Details of where each child will be living.

1 ....

2 ....

3 ....

4 ....

5 ....

6 ....

Dates

The date and place you and your **spouse** married.

The date and place you and your spouse last lived together.

Housing

Will you remain in the family home?

Yes

Is the rent or mortgage being paid?

Yes – fine, but don't be complacent. Tell your council, housing association, landlord or building society what has happened and ask to be notified if your **spouse** stops paying.

No – tell your council, housing association, landlord or building society *now* and ask for advice.

Can you afford to pay the rent/mortgage yourself?

Yes – fine, but try to get your spouse to contribute, especially if there are children involved.

No – if your spouse cannot or will not contribute, ask about housing benefit/income support – see Department for Work and Pensions (DWP) in 'Useful Contacts', p 164). Ask the building society to let you make lower repayments until you sort yourself out.

Meanwhile, try to get your spouse to pay. You may qualify for **Legal Help** to do this (see Chapter 10).

Will you remain in the family home?

No

Have you got somewhere else to live?

Yes – fine. Remember that you may qualify for housing benefit even for private rentals.

No – tell the council or housing association now and ask for advice. Provision varies, so we cannot generalise.

1   If one of you leaves the family home, they need to tell:

o   the building society or bank (that is, the mortgage lender) if your home is mortgaged;

o   the landlord if you live in private rented accommodation;

o   the council or housing association if you live in council or housing association property.

They need to know, and your **spouse** may not bother to inform them. It is also a good idea to tell the following:

o   Council Tax office (the one left behind may qualify for Council Tax relief);

o   water supplier;

o   electricity supplier;

o   gas supplier.

It is sensible to do this yourself in case your spouse forgets – or deliberately neglects – this chore.

2   *Protecting the family home*

People can do strange things if they are under a lot of stress, and marriage breakdown is one of the most stressful things that can happen to you. So we will mention here the importance of protecting your stake in the family home to make sure that your spouse does not dispose of it while your back is turned! Even if the family home is owned (or rented – the principle is the same) in your spouse's sole name, you have **matrimonial home rights** (or 'rights of occupation' - both terms are in current use) and you can also make sure they do not sell or otherwise dispose of it without your permission. We tell you how to do this – see p 116.

Money

Can you afford to keep yourself (and the children)?

Yes – fine, but your **spouse** has responsibilities. Try to get them to contribute – especially if there are children.

Consider contacting the **Child Support Agency (CSA)** (see 'Useful Contacts', p 166) for an unofficial assessment of how much they should be paying.

No – ask about income support, or working family tax credit if you are working. After April 2003, the system of tax credits changed and we provide more details of the new system on p 108 (see also Department for Work and Pensions (DWP) in 'Useful contacts', p 164).

You may also qualify for an emergency loan to help, for example, with the cost of moving house. Note that if you have children, and if you apply for benefits, the DWP will automatically send a Child Support Agency form. They take the view that it is better for a **non-resident parent** to support the children than the state.

Have you a joint bank or building society account?

Yes – quick! – make sure your spouse can't draw out all the money (at the risk of seeming cynical, might we suggest you consider getting your share out first?). Or ask the bank not to honour any transactions unless both of you have signed.

No – lucky you! But check any other joint assets to make sure your spouse can't dispose of those (see 'Protecting the family home', p 27).

What about the family car? Consider putting the vehicle registration document in a very safe place until the future of the car has been decided.

Have you a bank or building society account of your own?

Yes – congratulations. You are going to need it.

No – open one now.

Draft Separation Agreement

Below is a draft Separation Agreement. It is not exhaustive and you would certainly need to change some items to suit your own circumstances.

We recommend that you write down the main points you have agreed with your **spouse**, perhaps using our questionnaire in Chapter 5 as a starting point. Make sure that:

o   you really *have* reached an agreement and that there are no misunderstandings or hidden doubts;

o   you have got all your financial information together (you may like to use the financial form at www.courtservice.gov.uk/cms/forms.htm);

o   you have been frank with each other about your assets.

If it comes to court proceedings later, you will both have to disclose all your financial affairs and openness now could save a lot of unpleasantness later.

Spend time now, save money later

Remember that lawyers charge mainly on the basis of time spent – so anything that makes it easier, and therefore quicker, for them to handle your case will automatically save you money.

If, in the future, you need to instruct a solicitor about the financial side of your marriage breakdown (and you will almost certainly need one if your affairs are at all complicated), any work you put in now is likely to reduce the amount of time your solicitor needs to spend on your case. This draft Agreement is designed to make things easy for a solicitor if you instruct one.

You will see that the draft Agreement is in two parts: 'Background' (which is much shorter) and 'Operative provisions'. The 'Background' sets out who you are, when and where you married and your children's names. All of this information is required if you decide to **divorce**. The 'Operative provisions', on the other hand, spell out the terms of the agreement itself. Your solicitor will be able to use the information in this draft Separation Agreement when, for example, it is time to draw up a **Consent Order**.

In the meantime our Separation Agreement, though not legally binding, addresses all the issues that are likely to arise. Some points in the Agreement may not apply to you. In that case, delete them and renumber the remaining clauses.

We have provided for the Agreement to be witnessed, to impress upon you and your **spouse** that although it might not stand up in a court of law, *you* are meant to stick to it. It should, if you are both sincere about this, be sufficient to tide you over until:

o you actually divorce; *or*

o you decide to live together again.

Note that the Agreement automatically comes to an end if:

o one of you dies;

o you resume living together;

o any court order is made to cancel or vary the terms of the agreement; or

o both of you agree in writing to end or vary the agreement.

Separation Agreement

[Note that we have called you Spouse 1 and Spouse 2. When you come to 'personalise' your Agreement, replace Spouse 1 and Spouse 2 with your forenames.]

THIS SEPARATION AGREEMENT is made the .... day of .... 200[ ]

between:

Spouse 1: *[full name]* ....

of *[address]* ....

and:

Spouse 2: *[full name]* ....

of *[address]* ....

Background

(1)   *[Spouse 1]* and *[Spouse 2]*

were married on *[date]* at *[place]*

[Copy this from the marriage certificate. It has to be absolutely correct.]

(2)   The following are children of/children adopted by both *[Spouse 1]* and *[Spouse 2]* or are children of the family *[this refers to stepchildren]*

[Insert children's names and ages.]

1   ....   DOB   ....

2   ....   DOB   ....

3   ....   DOB   ....

4   ....   DOB   ....

5   ....   DOB   ....

6   ....   DOB   ....

(3)   Differences have arisen between *[Spouse 1]* and *[Spouse 2]* which make it difficult for them to live together as a couple. They have therefore agreed to live separately and apart.

Operative provisions

1 *[Spouse 1]* and *[Spouse 2]* agree that:

1.1 They will live apart as if unmarried.

1.2 Each will be responsible for their own financial affairs and for the outgoings of their own home while living apart but remaining married.

The Inheritance (Provision for Family and Dependants) Act 1975 (see clause 1.3 below) states that if you die without making reasonable financial provision for your family and dependants, they can make a claim on your estate. Also 'dependants' include your ex-**spouse**, unless:

ɔ they have remarried; *or*

ɔ a court order has excluded their rights under the Act.

This is why it is vital to get a court to 'bless' any financial settlement (see 'A note on Consent Orders', p 103).

1.3 Each will waive all rights to each other's assets under the Inheritance (Provision for Family and Dependants) Act 1975.

1.4 Neither will make a claim on the other's property or claim a lump sum when the clauses in this Agreement have been complied with.

1.5 The distribution of the contents of the former family home has already been agreed, and each will collect their share upon completion of all the transactions set out in this Agreement.

1.6 In the event of both parties agreeing to a divorce, the court will be invited to make a **Consent Order** in the terms of this Agreement so far as property and finance are concerned.

1.7 Each party will pay their own legal costs, if any.

The clause below stops you from running up bills in each other's names and makes each of you liable only for their own expenses.

2   *[Spouse 1]* agrees:

2.1   That s/he will not enter into any credit arrangements in *[Spouse 2]*'s name.

2.2   That subject to *[Spouse 2]* making the payments referred to in clause 3, *[Spouse 1]* will maintain him/herself, and will indemnify *[Spouse 2]* from all other liabilities incurred in respect of him/herself.

(The clause below applies only where there is a family limited company. In practice, if this applies to you, *you will certainly need to seek professional advice*. If it does not apply to you, delete this clause and renumber the other clauses accordingly.)

2.3   That they will give up all interest in *[name of company]* Limited, transfer his/her shares to *[Spouse 2]* and produce a letter resigning as director and company secretary confirming that they have no claim against the company for loss of office or otherwise and that they are not liable for any future company debt.

*[Obviously the clause below, which allows one **spouse** to take on responsibility for the mortgage of the family home, would not apply if you lived in rented property. If it does not concern you, delete and renumber. If it does apply to you, remember to inform the building society.]*

2.4   That subject to the consent of the *[name of mortgage lender, eg, Moir's Bank or Border Building Society]* they will take over sole responsibility for the mortgage on the former family home at .... *[address]* and procure the release of *[Spouse 2]* from all liability for this.

[The clause below applies to cars on hire purchase. If it does not apply to you, delete and renumber.]

2.5   That upon *[Spouse 2]* discharging the outstanding finance thereon, and upon *[Spouse 2]* indemnifying *[Spouse 1]* in respect thereof, *[Spouse 1]* will indemnify *[Spouse 2]* from all further liabilities incurred in respect of the car reg no ....

(The clause below refers to property transfer and insurance policies. *If this applies to you, you must seek legal advice.* Property transfer is not a DIY matter. Apart from anything else, have you got your sums right?)

3   *[Spouse 2]* agrees:

3.1   That in return for the sum of .... pounds in cash [and the benefit of *[name of insurance company]* Life Endowment Policies Nos .... and .... *[Spouse 2]* will transfer to *[Spouse 1]* all his/her legal and beneficial interest in the former matrimonial home at .... *[address]*.

[The clauses below provide for maintenance for the children, including help with occasional needs such as school trips. They allow the level of maintenance to be reviewed without affecting the rest of the Agreement.]

3.2   That until the first of the events referred to in clause 5 below, *[Spouse 2]* will pay .... pounds per calendar month in respect of maintenance for *[children's names]*, the first payment to become due on the signing and completion of this Agreement.

3.2.1 The above figure is to be reviewed from time to time in the light of the prevailing financial climate and the children's changing needs.

3.2.2 *[Spouse 2]* will in addition to the .... pounds per calendar month pay *[Spouse 1]* on request such sums as may from time to time be required for the children's school trips while they are of primary school age.

When the children attend secondary school *[Spouse 1]* and *[Spouse 2]* will each bear one half of the cost of such trips.

[The clause below deals with the family car; A hands it over to B without charge. Remember to inform the DVLC and the car insurers.]

3.2.3 That *[Spouse 2]* will for a nil consideration give up all interest in the car registration no ....

[The clause below allows the spouse leaving the former family home to use that address for their mail until they are settled somewhere else.]

4   *[Spouse 2]* may if they wish use the former family home at .... *[address]* as an accommodation address for his/her mail until such time as *[Spouse 2]* purchases or rents a permanent home, *[Spouse 2]* to provide *[Spouse 1]* with stamped addressed envelopes for the purpose if mail is to be forwarded.

5   This Agreement ends automatically if:

5.1 *[Spouse 1]* dies;

5.2 *[Spouse 2]* dies;

5.3 *[Spouse 1]* and *[Spouse 2]* resume living together;

5.4 any court order is made to cancel or vary the payments agreed above;

5.5 both *[Spouse 1]* and *[Spouse 2]* agree in writing to terminate or to vary this Agreement.

IN WITNESS OF WHICH both parties have signed below

SIGNED BY ....

in the presence of *[witness name]* ....

SIGNED BY ....

in the presence of *[witness name]* ....

at *[witness address]* ....

[The witness does not need to know what is in the document. Witnesses witness the signing, not the document itself.]

7

You and your solicitor

If you do decide to instruct a solicitor – and you will need to do so unless you are homeless, penniless and childless – you need one who is right for you. You could be spending quite a lot of money, so you should treat this matter like any other major purchase and do your homework.

People often have unrealistic expectations about their solicitors. Here are some of the things your solicitor should *not* be:

○ *A counsellor.*

You are there for hard-headed practical advice, not therapy! All good solicitors have acquired some counselling skills along the way, but that is not what you are there for, and at £100 or more an hour this is a very expensive shoulder to cry on!

○ *A champion to fight for you, right or wrong.*

A good solicitor should give you sensible, balanced advice, not tell you what you would like to hear. If you are wrong, they should tell you so.

○ *A friend.*

Do not confuse a friendly, sympathetic manner with friendship. There needs to be professional detachment for the good of both of you. Keeping things on a professional level will also save you money. Save your intimate chats for your personal friends, who are not charging by the hour!

Shopping around

Beware! The solicitor who did a superb job of conveyancing for your brother-in-law may not be your best choice for family law.

Solicitors, like doctors, have their specialties. Many solicitors who specialise in family law are members of the Solicitors Family Law Association (SFLA), an association of solicitors who are 'committed to promoting a non-confrontational atmosphere in which family law matters are dealt with in a sensitive, constructive and cost-effective way'.

Many family lawyers are also members of the Law Society Family Law Panel. Membership of the SFLA and/or the Family Law Panel is a good indicator that a solicitor has a good level of expertise in this area of the law. For example, co-author Jane Moir is a member of both bodies.

○ Telephone or click onto the SFLA website (see 'Useful contacts', p 165) for details of SFLA solicitors near you. The SFLA believes that family break-up need not be a battle with winners and losers, but rather a search for a fair solution for everyone.

○ *Yellow Pages*. Flip through the directory under 'Solicitors'.

○ The Law Society (see 'Useful contacts', p 163) keeps regional directories of solicitors.

○ Word of mouth: ask around any friends who have been through a similar experience.

○ Surf the internet. Try typing in 'family law', '**divorce**' and 'family **mediation**' and remember to press the button to limit your search to the UK! You could try adding your locality (for example, East Anglia) to limit it still further.

Check them out

In any case, you need to check the firm out for yourself. You would not engage a builder or a childminder without vetting them, would you? Here are some points to look for. Even if you expect to be **publicly funded**, you are entitled to a good service for the **Legal Services Commission's** money.

All solicitors must follow a client care code and you should, when you instruct one, receive a **client care letter**. We include a typical client care letter on p 147. If you do not receive one, this is a strong indication that you should be looking elsewhere. Meanwhile, before you sign up with anyone, ask yourself:

ɔ *How efficiently did the reception desk handle your first contact?*

   If you were unimpressed, remember that although the receptionist is a guide to the overall efficiency of the firm, the solicitor sitting upstairs may nevertheless be an inspired whizz kid. It is sometimes unwise to judge by first appearances.

ɔ *How approachable is the solicitor or legal executive (see below) allocated to your case?*

   Good family solicitors are sympathetic and supportive, while maintaining a reassuring professional detachment. If you can't talk freely to the person allocated to your case, you are going to find the proceedings very stressful.

ɔ *What are the offices like?*

   Scruffy, untidy, unattractive offices suggest a general lack of care and respect for both staff and clients. The offices of good family lawyers are usually family-friendly. They will provide magazines for the adults and books and a toy box for children – and a supply of tissues for you if you burst into tears while telling your tale of woe! We know of one firm that made such a hit with a little girl that, long after the family's problems had been sorted out, the child stopped at the office door and demanded to 'go in and play'.

Need it always be a solicitor?

Many law firms employ family lawyers who are not qualified solicitors. Legal executives – often educated to degree level – are likely to be every bit as knowledgeable and efficient as solicitors in their chosen corner of the field, and their hourly charging rates may be lower.

Your first interview

Different solicitors have different techniques, but you should come armed with as much potentially useful information as possible. All the following information will be required at some time during the proceedings. For example, the marriage certificate and all the details about the children will be required for any **divorce petition**.

o   Marriage certificate.

o   Dates of birth for you, your **spouse** and any children.

o   Contact details, including home and work telephone numbers and e-mail addresses (if you have them) for you and your spouse.

o   Job details for you and your spouse.

o   Your National Insurance number and that of your spouse.

o   Details of the children's schools.

o   Dates and places of any previous marriages, both for you and your spouse.

o   If you are already separated, the date you separated.

o   Any official correspondence, such as from the **Child Support Agency** (**CSA**), from your spouse's solicitors or from your mortgage lender.

You are also going to be asked about your financial details. Prepare a summary, including details of:

o   your income;

o   your spouse's income;

o   any welfare benefits (bring the books along);

o   approximate value of the family home together with details of any mortgages, etc.

Copies of any financial documentation, such as pay slips and bank statements, are always helpful. You might also have a stab at completing the financial form available at www.courtservice.gov.uk/cms/forms.htm. It is all useful information for your solicitor. Before you hand anything over to your solicitor, make copies for your own file.

1   Supplying all the required information, and presenting it in an organised way, will save your solicitor time and you money.

2   Take a pen and notepad with you and take notes. If you are feeling stressed you may not take information on board, or be able to remember it later, unless you write it down. All lawyers take notes routinely and put the notes on their client's file. Careful note-taking is a good habit to get into in all your dealings. This applies especially to your dealings with officialdom, where you might not speak to the same person twice and someone may even refuse to believe you called at all unless you can supply dates and names!

Complaints

What if you are not satisfied with the way your solicitor handles your case?

All solicitors must provide a set complaints procedure.

ɔ   Your **client care letter** will tell you whom to approach first with any concerns – usually the person handling your case.

ɔ   If you cannot resolve the problem by raising the matter with the person dealing with your case, then take the matter to the senior partner (or whoever is named in the client care letter as the person in overall charge with particular responsibility to listen to and deal with complaints). This person will try to put matters right.

ɔ   If you are still not satisfied, you have the right to complain to the Office for the Supervision of Solicitors (see 'Useful contacts', p 163, for further details).

8

Emergencies: domestic violence

So far, we have dealt mainly with couples who separate by agreement – either formal or informal. However miserable they may feel about the break-up, they have at least set some ground rules and mean to stick by them. Nobody has been blatantly unreasonable.

Some people, however, have separation thrust upon them. They need short term protection – from violence, the threat of violence, harassment, sexual abuse or homelessness – and they need it *now*.

Domestic violence is what the law calls violence between married couples past or present, people who have had a relationship and those who are or have been cohabiting. You may apply for **a non-molestation order** or an **occupation order** under Part IV of the Family Law Act 1996 if your relationship to the **Respondent** is:

ɔ   married to them;

ɔ   formerly married to them;

ɔ   cohabiting with them;

ɔ   formerly cohabiting with them;

ɔ   both of you live or have lived in the same household;

ɔ   you are related, in which case you have to state how you are related;

ɔ   you have agreed to marry, in which case you have to state:

    –   the date you agreed to marry; *and*

    –   if that agreement has ended, the date when it ended;

o   both of you are the parents of a child and the other has **parental responsibility** for that child;

o   one of you is a parent of a child and the other has parental responsibility for that child;

o   one of you is the natural parent or grandparent of a child adopted or in the process of being adopted by that person;

o   you are both already involved in the same set of family court proceedings.

Domestic violence is loosely defined as violence against a person by another person with whom that person is, or has been, in a domestic relationship.

Sadly, domestic violence is all too common – up to a quarter of all *reported* crimes belong to this category. A violent incident may be as horrific as any car crash or pub brawl, but there are not usually any witnesses apart from the children and many incidents go unreported.

Forget the stereotypes; domestic violence is:

o   found in all classes of society; and

o   not confined to men beating up women.

It is often related to:

o   drink;

o   drugs;

o   a history of violence suffered in childhood;

o   the emotional stress of separating or **divorcing**.

Domestic violence can include:

o   physical abuse, including slapping, pushing and physical assault of any kind as well as more serious assaults;

o   sexual abuse;

o   psychological abuse (to put it cynically, this is where some women may come into their own);

o   threats of physical, sexual or psychological abuse;

o   intimidation;

o   harassment;

o   extreme and frequent verbal abuse;

o   damage to property, if it makes someone fear for their safety.

Additionally, allowing a child to witness any of these things, or putting the child at risk of witnessing them, can amount to child abuse.

Get help – fast!

1   If you are the violent one in such a situation, you need to do something about it at once. If you are honest with yourself, you will probably have some idea of why you are behaving like this. Consider moving out of the family home until you have sorted yourself out, whether by approaching an appropriate organisation, such as Alcoholics Anonymous, or asking your doctor to refer you for counselling. Don't wait until someone is badly hurt and you get arrested.

2   If you are the victim in this kind of situation, you need immediate help, either from the police (see below), or from a solicitor, who will help you to get an **injunction** in the **county court** to protect you and your children (see below).

Whether you are Punch or Judy in this situation, getting protection from domestic violence is not a DIY matter.

The professionals

Police

We have put the police first here because domestic violence is not a nine-to-five occurrence and the police, unlike most solicitors and social workers, are available 24 hours a day!

In the past, the police had a reputation for not taking 'domestics' seriously. Times are changing, however. Some police authorities automatically investigate and record all reported incidents of domestic violence, and some offer help and support to the victims too. Studies abroad have shown that in areas where the police take a strong line on domestic violence, the number of incidents drops.

If an actual assault has taken place, the police may consider whether to bring criminal charges: some police forces automatically seek to prosecute in such cases.

Solicitor

A solicitor can help you to obtain an **injunction** from the court to protect you and the children and you should contact one without delay.

Consider staying overnight with a friend or in a refuge (see 'Should you leave home?', below) if you cannot get an appointment with a solicitor that day, but most solicitors treat genuine emergency work very seriously and will move heaven and earth to squeeze you in urgently (see below for more details).

In some places, solicitors have got together to run a kind of domestic violence hotline to give victims access to professional advice out of office hours. Your local Citizens Advice Bureau (or, out of office hours, the police) should be able to tell you about any such scheme in your area.

Local authority housing departments

Your local authority housing department (see your local telephone directory) should be able to help with emergency accommodation if you are made homeless. Generally you will be given priority treatment, especially if you have children. However, it could still take weeks for the local authority to re-house you and they frequently resort to bed and breakfast type accommodation in urgent cases. Local authority practices vary widely, depending on the level of need and quantity of local authority housing in each area. Your solicitor will probably know whom to approach.

The Women's Aid Federation

The Women's Aid Federation can also help you to find a safe haven in an emergency. You can call their national 24-hour helpline or access their website (see 'Useful contacts', p 167). The Federation describes itself as 'England's national charity for women and children experiencing physical, sexual or emotional abuse in the home' (see 'Consider a refuge', below).

Meanwhile:

o   *Don't* take risks, especially if you have children at home.

o   *Don't* try to handle it yourself.

o   *Do* call in the professionals – without delay.

Should you leave home?

Not unless you have to. You should try to stay in the family home. There are tactical as well as practical reasons for this, as any solicitor will tell you, but in a dire emergency you may have no choice but to get out, at least for a day or two. In fact, if staying at home means your safety and well-being are under threat, you could be safer to leave – but if possible always ask a solicitor first, to find out about your rights in this situation.

---

1   If you do leave home because of violence and you have children, take them with you, because:

o   the children will be safer with you; and

o   you will have a higher priority for emergency accommodation if the need arises.

2   If you think you may qualify for **Legal Help** (see Chapter 10), you *must* bring your National Insurance details and benefit books with you, because:

o   your solicitor will need to see them to get Legal Help for you; and

o   you will need them to get money if you are away from home for any length of time.

Consider a refuge

If you do decide to leave home, you may be lucky enough to have a friend to stay with for a night or two, but what if your violent **spouse** finds out where you are and threatens your friend as well?

If you manage to consult a solicitor quickly and, between you, you obtain a court **injunction**, it will normally be your violent spouse who will have to leave home. But suppose it's Friday evening and the courts are closed until Monday morning?

At times like that, the Women's Aid Federation can help (see above and 'Useful contacts' for details).

If you do log onto the Women's Aid website, your secret is safe with them. The home page has a special button labelled 'Before using this site. Warning! If you are worried about someone knowing you have visited this website please click here'.

Women's Aid offers a nationwide network of safe houses for women and children. It also offers legal advice and links with other organisations.

Erin Pizzey, who played a major role in setting up Women's Aid, wrote a wonderful book (published by Penguin but now sadly out of print) called *Scream Quietly or the Neighbours Will Hear*. Anyone who thinks that victims of domestic violence somehow bring it upon themselves should try to borrow this book from their local library.

Can you change the locks?

You might feel that changing the locks would be a smart move to bar your violent **spouse** from the family home. There are two answers here, the official one and the unofficial one.

Officially, if you and your spouse own or rent your home jointly you have no legal right to lock them out. If you did change the locks, your spouse could, in theory at least, get a court to order you to give them access to the family home.

On the other hand, *you* could apply to the court for an **injunction** to make them leave. If your spouse's violent conduct is serious enough, the judge will make the order (see Chapter 9). After that you will be within your rights to change the locks. Your solicitor will explain all this.

Unofficially, it could be worth changing the locks anyway, to give you some respite until your spouse can obtain an order from the court – and if they did apply, you would be given the chance to oppose it.

Emergencies: going to court

See a solicitor

In a real emergency there is no realistic alternative to instructing a solicitor to go to court to get an **injunction** – a court order to protect you from your **spouse's** violent **behaviour** and/or bar your spouse from the family home. You may need to go to court with your papers in one hand and your solicitor in the other. Hopefully by the end of the day you will have your injunction, often with police powers attached (which means the police can arrest your spouse if they try it on again).

Make an appointment to see a solicitor at once, stressing that it is a domestic violence matter. Experienced family lawyers keep an 'injunction kit' ready with all the paperwork to enable them to give emergency clients a swift and effective service.

There is a lot of paperwork, especially if you are being **publicly funded** (see Chapter 10). Your solicitor is likely to ask you the following questions:

o   Has there ever been any violence between you and your spouse before?

o   Has either of you ever hurt the other?

o   Are you afraid of your spouse?

Your solicitor is also likely to ask you:

o   Has your spouse ever become violent after drinking alcohol or taking drugs?

o   Does your spouse lose their temper?

o   Do you ever lose your temper?

o   Do you often argue, and how often do your arguments end in violence?

All these questions are important because your solicitor must show the judge that you have a good case: making a court order is a serious matter.

Don't be afraid of being frank. Remember that it is difficult to shock a family solicitor, who will unfortunately have heard stories like yours many times before.

Medical evidence

If you have been injured, or even just bruised or grazed, you should show your injuries to your solicitor. They may arrange for you to be seen by a doctor and have a medical report prepared. This can provide useful evidence in court.

Many solicitors take Polaroid photographs of their clients' injuries. As one old lawyer said, 'Time is a great healer and bruises fade quickly. If there's another **hearing** a week or so after the first, it's as well to remind the judge what you looked like just after you were beaten up'.

Another possibility is a photo booth – provided of course that you can actually present your injury to the camera. A black eye is all very well, but you might have trouble photographing a bruised shoulder blade.

What kind of order?

An **injunction** is an order from a court saying either 'Oi – do this or else!' or 'Oi – cut that out or else!' Disobeying an injunction can lead to imprisonment. There are two kinds of order in domestic violence cases:

o   a **non-molestation order**;

o   an **occupation order**.

A non-molestation order forbids your **spouse** to assault or otherwise molest you or the children.

What precisely is 'molestation'? It can include pestering (such as nuisance phone calls) and general harassment as well as actual violence.

An occupation order tells your spouse to leave home and not come within a specified distance of it, such as 100 metres. If you have left home in fear of violence, an occupation order can also order your violent spouse to leave so that you can move back into your home. The judge has to look at each case very carefully before deciding whether to make an occupation order. They will try to find out whether the violent spouse has got somewhere to go before formally barring them from the family home.

Your solicitor will decide which order is needed. Practically speaking, if the incident is serious, your solicitor will apply for a non-molestation order *ex parte* (see below) to give immediate protection.

In our experience, many violent spouses tend to move out of the family home soon after having a non-molestation order served on them. As few judges would make an occupation order without notice (well, would *you* order someone out of their home without giving them a chance to tell their side of the story?), a non-molestation order is the logical way to get immediate protection.

A note on children

In some cases it is the children, rather than a **spouse**, who are at risk. In those cases, a court can make an order to keep the violent spouse away from the children. If this applies to you, your local social services department might get involved. However, you should always contact the police first because they are available 24 hours a day, seven days a week.

Ex parte – no notice

We mentioned notice above. Usually if you take someone to court, whether for debt, injunction proceedings or anything else, the **Respondent** (the one who is being sued; the person doing the suing is called the **Applicant**) is given notice of the date of the **hearing** so that they can turn up in court and tell their side of the story.

In some – usually fairly mild – domestic violence cases, your application for an injunction might be 'on notice', in which case the papers must be **served** on your spouse at least two working days before the hearing. Your solicitor will see to this for you.

Often in emergency situations, however, the judge will allow your solicitor to help you to apply for a **non-molestation order** to restrain a violent spouse without requiring anyone to inform your spouse. This is often called an *ex parte* order and to make it legally binding, the order, once the judge has signed it, has to be served on – that is, handed to – your spouse.

Have no fear! You will *not* have to do this yourself. Your solicitor will arrange this for you. Note that there will be a sort of return match – a hearing on notice (*inter partes*) with your spouse present in court – a week or so later, but in the interim period you will be protected.

In certain circumstances where it is reasonable for you not to let your **spouse** know where you are staying, or if you are making the application on behalf of a child, you will not need to put your address on the application form. Instead, you can give your address to the court on a special form that they supply.

What happens in court?

Your solicitor will get an application typed up for you to sign before you go to court. You will have to make and sign a statement in support of your application, which your solicitor will also prepare on your behalf.

We can't tell you in detail what will happen when you get to court, as customs vary, but you will have your solicitor or a barrister with you.

Courts are like doctors' surgeries – they squeeze in emergencies as best they can, but you may still have a longish wait to be seen. Try, if at all possible, to leave the children with a friend who can care for them for as long as it takes, which could be all day. If you have to bring them, bring something to keep them amused. There will be lavatories and a drinks machine near the waiting area, but little else. Take something to read; the reading matter in the court anteroom may not be to your taste!

The hearing

Your case will probably be heard in the judge's chambers, which in practice means a book-lined room with a desk for the judge and a table and chairs for other people. In an *ex parte* **hearing** only you, the judge and your solicitor or barrister will be there.

Your solicitor or barrister will speak for you, but if the judge does address you directly, you should call them 'Your Honour'.

If all goes well, the judge will make the order. There may be a short wait while it is typed up, then your solicitor will get the order **served** on:

o   your **spouse;** and

o   the local police, if the order includes police powers.

If your order is made *ex parte* there will be a second hearing on **notice**, usually about a week later. This enables your spouse to get legal advice and present their side of the story.

The second hearing will be held in the judge's chambers as before. This time your spouse and their solicitor will be there too. The judge may confirm the order, or your spouse might be allowed to give **undertakings** (promises) to the court that they will behave. Breaking an undertaking to a court is just as serious as breaking a court order.

Interlude: if you are the violent one

Don't wait until you have lashed out at your **spouse** and been **served** with an **injunction** or ordered to attend a court **hearing**. Consider moving out of the family home for a cooling-off period before any real harm is done.

If you do receive an injunction, or **notice** that your spouse has applied for one, read it carefully along with any other paperwork that comes with it. Then see a solicitor as soon as possible. You may be eligible for free advice under the **Legal Help Scheme** (see Chapter 10).

The solicitor will help you to make a statement to send to the court. This statement is an **affidavit** and you will have to **swear** that it is true. You might be able to avoid having an order made if you give **undertakings** to the court that you will behave yourself in future.

Afterword: the costs

Never let lack of money put you off instructing a solicitor. Help is available (see Chapter 10). It applies equally to non-urgent matters, such as financial settlements and disputes over children, but it is particularly important in an emergency.

10

Legal help and public funding

The **Legal Help Scheme** is not only for emergencies, although you may first come across it in an emergency situation. It is available to anyone who needs legal advice and/or assistance and who cannot afford to pay for it.

A first aid dressing

What people need in an emergency is first aid. Many solicitors offer needy clients first aid free of charge in the form of **Legal Help**. This used to be called the Green Form Scheme (see 'Time for trivia', p xvii) because the form that solicitors and their clients signed was green. The form tells the **Legal Services Commission** (**LSC**) who you are and what your solicitor did for you. Afterwards your solicitors can send the form in to the LSC and claim their fee from public money.

Since April 2001, Legal Help has been *automatically* available only to people who receive:

o   income support; *or*

o   income-based job seeker's allowance.

You may, however, also be eligible if you receive:

o   families tax credit; or

o   disabled person's tax credit.

In some cases, if you get less than the maximum credits (see above), you may still qualify for Legal Help. A solicitor will be able to advise.

If you are not receiving any of these benefits a solicitor will, either free of charge or for a very modest fee, take a swift look at your income and capital to see whether you qualify for **Legal Help**.

Good news!

A client who is separated from their **spouse** is considered as a single person. So, even if you are married to a millionaire, if you haven't got much money of your own you may well qualify for **Legal Help**.

This is a very simplified view of the Legal Help system. Your solicitor will soon tell you whether you qualify for Legal Help. If you qualify, your solicitor can do a certain amount of work for you free of charge, which would normally include preparing and issuing a **divorce petition**.

For anything more, they may be able to get permission to extend the time they can spend on your case, but it is more likely that they will need to apply for **public funding** (see below) for you, particularly if they need to represent you in court, such as on **ancillary relief** (see p 106) or what a client of ours called, memorably, 'one of them violent seductions' – a domestic violence **injunction**.

Public funding (formerly called 'legal aid')

If **Legal Help** is a first aid dressing, **public funding** is full medical care: hospital, X-rays, the lot. It is different from Legal Help in that there is a scale of contributions depending on your means.

If you qualify for Legal Help, you will not have to pay anything at all for public funding provided your financial situation remains the same throughout the proceedings. Otherwise, your contribution to your public funding will be calculated according to your financial situation.

There is plenty of paperwork. Your solicitor will have to fill in at least two many-paged forms – one for the legal merits of your case, another for your finances – to apply for public funding on your behalf. Your solicitor will, if possible, use the time available to them on your Legal Help form to finance the paperwork for public funding.

In a grave emergency, your solicitor will be able to fax an application for public funding there and then, and your paperwork will catch up later. In non-urgent cases, your application will work its way through the system until, if the application is successful, you will be sent an 'Offer', which (if you accept) will entitle you to full legal representation under your Certificate of Public Funding. The Offer will tell you how much you have to pay each month and also what work will be covered by your certificate.

How long does it take?

Legal Help is immediate – your solicitor will decide on the spot whether you qualify.

---

1   That's why you should always take your benefit book in to your initial meeting with your solicitor!

2   Take your marriage certificate with you. If you later start **divorce** proceedings, your solicitor will need the certificate and you may as well save yourself a journey now.

Normally Legal Help will be enough to cover the cost of obtaining a simple, straightforward **divorce** with no complications of any kind. You sign the application form for Legal Help and your solicitor does the rest of the paperwork; there is no waiting period.

A Certificate of Public Funding may, and usually does, take your solicitor more time to obtain on your behalf. In certain very limited circumstances, your solicitor can speed up the process. This will, however, only be possible in an emergency, such as where you need protection from a violent **spouse**, or if you have good reason to believe that your spouse may try to take the children out of the country.

Your Certificate of Public Funding, when it arrives, will say exactly what it covers. It may be limited to certain activities, such as investigative work, or it may have a wider scope. In some cases, it may cover everything that is necessary to finalise matters on your behalf. In other cases it will take you just so far along the road before your solicitor has to obtain confirmation from another solicitor or barrister that your case merits further work, and therefore public money, spending on it. This is not your problem; your solicitor will make sure their fees are covered.

The statutory charge

We know an old solicitor who used to explain the **statutory charge** as follows:

'Supposing I, through my skill, agility and daring, obtain X amount of money for you, or save you from losing X amount of money, do you agree – out of said X amount of money – to pay back to the **Legal Services Commission** the money they will have spent on your case?'

She would ask this several times during the proceedings to make sure the client understood the implications and could never plead ignorance if the statutory charge kicked in.

A more bureaucratic way of explaining the statutory charge is this: suppose that thanks to **public funding** you obtain assets or money, or recover some assets or money from your **spouse**, you must then pay your legal fees back to the government out of those assets or that money. This is called the statutory charge. It will also apply to assets and money which your spouse has claimed from you and which you have managed to hang on to.

Your solicitor should remind you about this several times and also hand you a leaflet about it, but we will spell it out now.

Public funding is like a loan from the Legal Services Commission; a loan that you don't need to repay unless you get – or keep – assets (money, property, etc). In that case you may have to pay back your loan, which will enable the Legal Services Commission (formerly the Legal Aid Board) to help someone else. You can pay it back in cash, or have a charge (like a mortgage) on your home. The statutory charge does not apply to the following cases:

○ if you do not gain or keep the property or money that was in dispute;

○ if you recover all your costs from the other side (if you recover some of your costs the statutory charge applies to the rest);

○ maintenance payments;

○ the first £3,000 of any money or property you gain or keep in **divorce** cases and most other family proceedings;

○ where your solicitor is advising you while you attend family **mediation**, under a 'Help with mediation' certificate;

○ where advice is given only under the **Legal Help Scheme**.

Normally the statutory charge has to be paid as soon as the money or property comes through from the other side. Usually payments have to be made through your solicitor, who will make the appropriate deductions and hand over any balance to you.

If you recover a home, or money to buy one, it may be possible to delay payment of the statutory charge. The charge is registered on the house (like a mortgage) and, again like a mortgage, interest will be charged. When you sell the house, the statutory charge will then have to be paid off just like an ordinary mortgage.

Divorce: how do I get one?

I want it to be final – how do I get a divorce?

You can forget high profile **divorce** cases and courtroom dramas. Actually getting a divorce is very low-key indeed. It is, broadly speaking, a matter of filling in the right forms and waiting for your file to work its way through the system. Our flowchart (pp 64–66) shows how it is done. You can begin the process of obtaining a divorce in any of the **county courts** listed on our website, but we recommend that you use your local court, which is usually the court nearest to you. The courts are open weekdays (not bank holidays) between 10 am and 4 pm, and they may be able to field telephone enquiries between 9 am and 5 pm.

Will I have to go to court?

Not in an open-and-shut case. You will not even know when your case will hit the judge's desk. While you get on with your daily life, the judge sits down with a pile of files and works through them. The judge OKs your application, and a few weeks later you are a single man or woman again.

Is that all there is to it?

No! Money, property, pension rights and so on are problems which must be dealt with, whether you are divorcing or just separating, but it is not the business of the judge who is actually processing your **divorce** papers to be concerned with your property or your money. That aspect is dealt with separately – the buzzword is **ancillary relief**. At the divorce stage, the judge just has to be satisfied that:

o   your marriage is over;

o   you have got the paperwork right;

o   any children involved will be properly looked after.

A judge who is happy about all three will sign a **Certificate of Entitlement to a Decree** (see p 148), saying when your **Decree Nisi** will be pronounced. Certificate of Entitlement? Decree Nisi? Don't get bogged down with unfamiliar expressions. Turn to 'Buzzwords' and trust us.

Divorce – a path through the maze

The fees we quote in this book were all correct at the time of writing, but nothing is permanent. Check out the Court Service website (see 'Useful contacts', p 161) for current fees. They also offer several free leaflets on **divorce** both online and from your local court or Citizens Advice Bureau (CAB).

Always check on the Court Service website that the form you are using is up-to-date: they can change without warning, as we found out when we were collecting the forms for this book!

Now post or take everything to your local court.

1   You can often save time and tears if you discuss the **Statement of Arrangements for Children** with your **spouse** before sending it to the court. Agree the arrangements and get your spouse to sign the Statement before sending your paperwork to the court.

Suppose your spouse receives the Statement of Arrangements along with the **divorce petition** and does not agree with them? The worst-case scenario could be a bitter struggle over the children, possibly involving several court appearances and a great deal of stress for everyone. Far better to ask the court to 'bless' arrrangements that both of you are content with.

2   In **'behaviour'** divorces, if your spouse is at all co-operative it is worth showing them the draft petition before sending it to the court, so that you can agree on the forms of words that are least objectionable to your spouse. A little give and take at this stage could save a good deal of hassle later. The Solicitors Family Law Association (SFLA) follows a code of practice which includes submitting the draft petition to the other side before issuing it in court.

For examples of 'behaviour', see Chapter 20. We have never met a **Respondent** who did not find an itemised description of their misdeeds and shortcomings hurtful, even if every word is true. Bluntly speaking, a spouse who has not been bad mouthed to the court is more likely to agree to a fair financial deal later.

Fortunately, it is possible to obtain a divorce on the basis of some very bland wording. That is why the SFLA suggests agreeing on the wording in advance.

3   As soon as the court gives you a case number, take a careful note of it and always quote it when you telephone or write to the court.

---

1   A solicitor will charge you a small **'swear** fee'. An officer of the court will not charge a fee.

2   Court bailiffs are a fine body of people, but they may be less ingenious at finding the **Respondent** than a professional process server. A process server will, for a modest fee, serve a **petition** and provide an **affidavit** to the effect that the petition has been duly served. Look in *Yellow Pages* under 'Process Servers'.

3   Whoever has to serve the petition, unless they know the Respondent by sight already, will find a recent photograph a big help. They will also find them more easily if you can give them some idea of the Respondent's movements during the day and in the evenings, for example, their times and place of work, or details of a public house or social club where they go during their leisure time. We have included this point in our letter on p 159 requesting bailiff service.

A path through the maze – stage 1

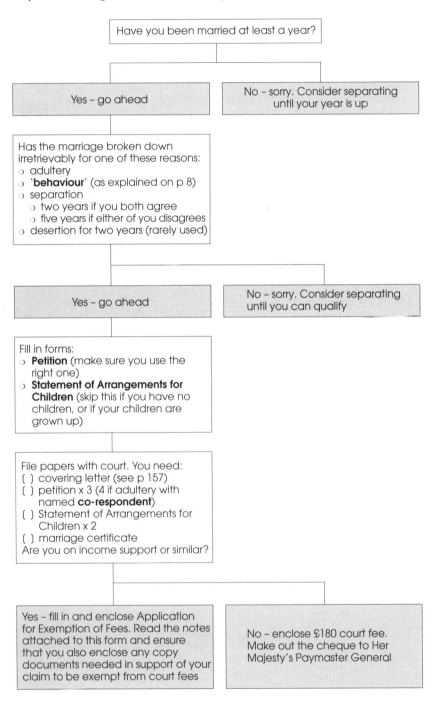

Have you been married at least a year?

Yes – go ahead

No – sorry. Consider separating until your year is up

Has the marriage broken down irretrievably for one of these reasons:
○ adultery
○ **behaviour** (as explained on p 8)
○ separation
　○ two years if you both agree
　○ five years if either of you disagrees
○ desertion for two years (rarely used)

Yes – go ahead

No – sorry. Consider separating until you can qualify

Fill in forms:
○ **Petition** (make sure you use the right one)
○ **Statement of Arrangements for Children** (skip this if you have no children, or if your children are grown up)

File papers with court. You need:
( ) covering letter (see p 157)
( ) petition x 3 (4 if adultery with named **co-respondent**)
( ) Statement of Arrangements for Children x 2
( ) marriage certificate
Are you on income support or similar?

Yes – fill in and enclose Application for Exemption of Fees. Read the notes attached to this form and ensure that you also enclose any copy documents needed in support of your claim to be exempt from court fees

No – enclose £180 court fee. Make out the cheque to Her Majesty's Paymaster General

A path through the maze – stage 2

> Did you get the paperwork right at that stage?

Yes – the court:
- sends petition and Statement of Arrangements for Children (if any) to the Respondent
- sends **Notice of Issue of Petition and Postal Service** to you confirming this has been done
- allocates a number to your case

No – sorry. The court sends the papers back to you, telling you where you went wrong. Try again after checking the website

Has the Respondent:
- signed an **Acknowledgement of Service** to confirm they have received the papers and is not defending?

and (if children are involved)
- signed the Statement of Arrangements for Children? (if not done previously – see 'Power point' above)

Yes – the court will send you:
- an Application for Directions for Trial
- a copy of the Acknowledgement of Service and
- an affidavit

No – you may need to ask the court bailiff to hand the papers to your **spouse** personally. This costs £10. See p 63 and the covering letter on p 158 and on the companion website

Fill in:
- the **Application for Directions for Trial**.
- the **affidavit**

Take affidavit and Acknowledgement of Service to a solicitor (who will charge a small fee) or an officer of the court (who will not charge a fee). Sign the affidavit in front of a solicitor or an officer of the court while **swearing** or **affirming** that you recognise the **Respondent's** signature on the Acknowledgement of Service and that you are telling the truth.

Send to the court:
- covering letter (see p 158)
- Application for Directions for Trial
- affidavit with the Acknowledgement of Service

A path through the maze – stage 3

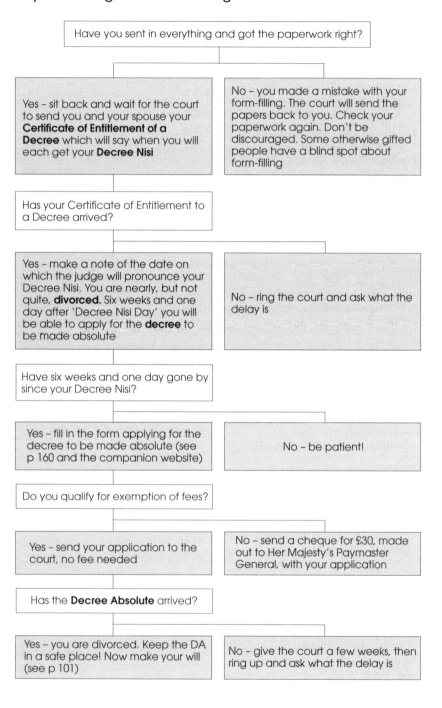

Have you sent in everything and got the paperwork right?

Yes – sit back and wait for the court to send you and your spouse your **Certificate of Entitlement of a Decree** which will say when you will each get your **Decree Nisi**

No – you made a mistake with your form-filling. The court will send the papers back to you. Check your paperwork again. Don't be discouraged. Some otherwise gifted people have a blind spot about form-filling

Has your Certificate of Entitlement to a Decree arrived?

Yes – make a note of the date on which the judge will pronounce your Decree Nisi. You are nearly, but not quite, **divorced**. Six weeks and one day after 'Decree Nisi Day' you will be able to apply for the **decree** to be made absolute

No – ring the court and ask what the delay is

Have six weeks and one day gone by since your Decree Nisi?

Yes – fill in the form applying for the decree to be made absolute (see p 160 and the companion website)

No – be patient!

Do you qualify for exemption of fees?

Yes – send your application to the court, no fee needed

No – send a cheque for £30, made out to Her Majesty's Paymaster General, with your application

Has the **Decree Absolute** arrived?

Yes – you are divorced. Keep the DA in a safe place! Now make your will (see p 101)

No – give the court a few weeks, then ring up and ask what the delay is

Tackling the paperwork

You can see from the flowcharts that, even with help and advice, **divorce** is far from instant! Few people would want it to be. Ending a marriage is not like selling a car or buying a hi-fi. There is a lot more form-filling, for one thing! Here we expand on the points in the diagrams.

Have you served your time?

In other words, have you been married for at least one year?

You cannot do anything unless:

ɔ   the marriage has broken down irretrievably; *and*

ɔ   you have served your time.

Less than one year of marriage means you cannot yet get a **divorce**. Possibly, in very exceptional circumstances, you can apply to get the marriage **annulled**, or you may apply for a **Decree** of **Judicial Separation**.

A **nullity** suit is not a DIY matter, however, and neither is a **Decree** of **Judicial Separation**. Seek professional advice.

After one year of marriage you can apply for a divorce for:

ɔ   **'behaviour'**; *or*

ɔ   adultery.

After two years apart, you can apply for a divorce on the grounds of two years' separation, with your **spouse's** consent.

After five years apart, you can go ahead with a five years' separation **petition** without your spouse's consent.

'Facts' for divorce

Before you start form-filling you will have to choose a 'fact', or reason, for divorcing. You may have heard people talk about *grounds* for **divorce**. The irretrievable breakdown of a marriage is the only *ground* for divorce. The different *facts* for divorce are:

- ɔ 'behaviour';
- ɔ adultery;
- ɔ two years' separation;
- ɔ five years' separation;
- ɔ desertion.

Most people will know which category they will fit into, but:

- ɔ if you have been deserted, use 'behaviour' instead, since the law regards deserting anyone as automatically unreasonable – which is the sort of behaviour you have to convince the court about – and 'behaviour' is easier to prove;

- ɔ **spouses** of serial adulterers (or adulteresses!) may prefer to cite 'behaviour' rather than try to list all the dates. In that case you would not use the word 'adultery', but something along the lines of the particulars in Chapter 20.

The petition form

Until very recently there was a different **divorce petition** form for each category. Now there is just one. In theory this simplifies matters but it does mean that your form-filling has to be spot on.

We print extracts from this form on pp 71–81 of this book, and you can download the form and the accompanying 'Notes for Guidance' from the Court Service website (see 'Useful contacts', p 161).

'Good form'

Here is an overview of the procedure you must follow.

1   Find the details of your local **county court** (look in your local telephone directory under 'Courts') and call them to check that our fees information is up to date (it was at the time of writing).

2   Dig out your marriage certificate.

If your marriage certificate has gone AWOL, don't panic! Replacement marriage certificates are obtainable from the Registrar for the district where the marriage took place or from the Registrar General in Southport (see 'FAQs' and 'Useful contacts', p 161).

3   Fill in and sign your **divorce petition** (see our notes on pp 71–81). Refer to the marriage certificate for the precise details of date and place of marriage.

4   Fill in and sign your **Statement of Arrangements for Children** – it is best if both parents sign this before filing with the court (see 'Power point' on p 62, above).

5   Write out a cheque for £180, payable to Her Majesty's Paymaster General *or* send form EX160 applying for exemption of fees – see 'Important note' below.

Important note

People on income support or family credit qualify for exemption of their court fees (we have included a sample form EX160 on the Court Service website) and send this instead of the £180 cheque. You can pick one up from your local court or download one from the Court Service website (see 'Useful contacts', p 161).

Free Legal Help?

If you have come straight to this chapter you may not realise that people on income support, family tax credit or very low incomes also qualify for free legal advice and assistance under the **Legal Help Scheme**. Consult a solicitor if you think you may qualify (see Chapter 10 for fuller details).

6   Write a covering letter to the court (see our sample on the companion website).

7   Open a (paper) file called 'Divorce'.

It will help you to organise your papers if within your divorce file you create two separate folders – one containing all the paperwork sent to and received from the court and another for correspondence between you and your **spouse** or their solicitors.

Now make:

o   three copies of the petition (four copies if there is a named **Co-respondent**);

o   two copies of the Statement of Arrangements for Children;

o   one copy of your marriage certificate, because you will never see the original again after filing your petition;

o   one copy of your covering letter.

Now send to the court:

o   the original petition + two copies (three copies if there is a Co-respondent);

o   the original Statement of Arrangements for Children + one copy;

o   the original marriage certificate;

o   your covering letter;

o   your cheque or form EX160.

Check everything carefully before sending it off, and keep one copy of everything in your file.

Form-filling is not everyone's strong point, but court officials are very good at it. Visit the court and show your paperwork to a friendly clerk to check you have got it right, rather than have it rejected.

Nit-picking accuracy

All the forms have to be completed in a very precise way. There are times when we suspect that court officials are carefully selected for their eagle eye and relentless pedantry as well as their form-filling skills. If you get anything wrong, the court will return your papers.

o   If the marriage certificate says 'The Church of St Margaret' don't think that 'St Margaret's Church' will do. It won't.

o   Likewise, you must take great care with names, dates and spellings. Your name and your spouse's name must be exactly as on the marriage certificate (even if the registrar got it wrong on the marriage certificate!).

Don't say we didn't warn you!

12

Filling in the petition

Now for some heavy duty form-filling.

'Behaviour' petition

Let's start with this one because it is the *least* straightforward **petition** to fill in. You are caught between a rock and a hard place. On the one hand, you need to convince a judge that your **spouse's behaviour** is such that 'the **Petitioner** cannot reasonably be expected to live with the **Respondent**'. On the other hand, you must avoid bruising your spouse's feelings so badly that they refuse to co-operate.

If your **spouse** *does* refuse to play ball, you could find yourself with a contested **divorce** on your hands, which is emphatically not a DIY matter: seek legal advice.

Before completing this form, read carefully the attached **Notes for Guidance**.

In the   **County Court***
                                                        *Delete as
                                                        appropriate
In the Principal Registry*   **No.**

In the .... County Court

Put in the name of your nearest **county court** that handles **divorces**. Check the address of your local court in the telephone directory.

Principal Registry

Cross this out unless you are petitioning in London and wish to use the High Court instead of your local **county court**.

No of Matter

Leave blank. The court will allocate a number to your case.

---

(1)   On the   day of   [19   ] [20   ] the petitioner

was lawfully married to

(hereinafter called "the

respondent") at

Section 1

On the [i] ...... day of [ii] ...... [iii] .... the petitioner [iv]
... was lawfully married to
[v] .... (hereinafter called 'the respondent')
at [vi] ....

You need to fill in:

(i), (ii), (iii) the day, month and year of your marriage;

(iv) your name (you are the **Petitioner**);

(v) your **spouse's** name (they are the **Respondent**);

(vi) the place of your marriage.

      (a)   If the marriage took place in a Register Office put:

          The Register Office, in the District of ....
          in the County of ....

      (b)   If the marriage took place in a church put:

          .... Church (get it right – see the note on p 70 above), in the Parish of .... in the County of ....

Copy this information from your marriage certificate. If either of you has had a change of name since then, you need to add either:

○   *Name changed by deed poll;* or

○   *Now known as* ....

| (2) | The petitioner and respondent last lived together as husband and wife at |

Section 2

The Petitioner and the Respondent last lived together as husband and wife at ....

Insert the address where you last lived together as a couple. If you are still occupying the same house, this does not matter.

| (3) | The court has jurisdiction under Article 2(1) of the Council Regulation on the following ground(s): |

Section 3

The Court has jurisdiction under Article 2(1) of the Council Regulation on the following ground(s):

This section is intended to prove to the court that it has **jurisdiction** in your case. Access the 'Notes for Guidance' that accompany every petition on the Court Service website – www. courtservice.gov.uk.

You need to insert *one* of the following paragraphs:

(a) The **Petitioner** and the **Respondent** are both habitually resident in England and Wales.

(b) The Petitioner and the Respondent were last habitually resident in England and Wales and the Petitioner/Respondent still resides there.

(c) The Respondent is habitually resident in England and Wales.

(d) The Petitioner is habitually resident in England and Wales and has resided there for at least one year immediately prior to the presentation of this petition. [*You should give the address(es) where you lived during that time and the length of time lived at each address.*]

(e) The Petitioner is domiciled and habitually resident in England and Wales and has resided there for at least six months immediately prior to the presentation of the petition. [*You should give the address(es) where you lived during that time and the length of time lived at each address.*]

(f)   The Petitioner and the Respondent are both domiciled in England and Wales.

The word *domicile* refers to the country that an individual treats as their permanent home and to which they have the closest legal ties. A person will either have a domicile of origin, which is the country of their birth, or a domicile of choice. It is not possible to have two domiciles. A person who chooses to have a permanent home elsewhere than where they were born may choose that country of residence to be their new domicile, but they will lose their domicile of origin. This can be a complicated issue. If you are in any doubt as to your domicile we recommend that you use one of the options (a) to (d) set out above instead. If you cannot use one of the other options and you are still uncertain as to your domicile, seek legal advice.

If you do not fall within any of the grounds stated above there is one final ground you may use, more details of which are given in the court's own 'Notes for Guidance'. If you need to resort to this last ground, then seek legal advice.

(4)	The petitioner is by occupation a	and resides at
	The respondent is by occupation a	and resides at

Section 4

The Petitioner is by occupation a ....

Put in your job (or 'Housewife', 'Retired' or whatever).

and resides at ....

Put in your current address.

The Respondent is by occupation a ....

Put in your **spouse's** job.

and resides at ....

Put in your spouse's current address.

(5)   There are no children of the family now living _except_

Section 5

*There are no children of the family now living **except** ....*

If you have no children, cross out *except*.

If you do have children, fill in after *except*:

ɔ   their full name(s) (including surnames);

ɔ   their date(s) of birth, or 'Over 18', if this is the case;

ɔ   if a child is over 16 but under 18, whether they are:

ɔ   at school;

ɔ   at college;

ɔ   training for a trade, profession or vocation; or

ɔ   working full-time.

(6)   No other child, now living, has been born to the petitioner/respondent during the marriage (so far as is known
to the petitioner) _except_

Section 6

*No other child, now living, has been born to the Petitioner/Respondent during the marriage so far as is known to the Petitioner **except** ....*

You need to delete either 'Petitioner' or 'Respondent'.

ɔ   If you are the **Petitioner** and also the wife, then delete **Respondent**.

ɔ   If you are the husband **petitioning** for **divorce**, then you need to delete the reference to Petitioner.

In other words, only the female can bear children, so this clause needs to be amended by deleting reference to the Petitioner if he is male or the Respondent if he is male, whichever is applicable in your divorce.

If there is a child, such as by an extra-marital relationship, living elsewhere, fill in:

ɔ   the child's full name (including surname); and

ɔ   their date of birth, or 'Over 18', if this is the case.

If there is any dispute about whether a child is a child of the family, please add a short paragraph saying so.

> (7) There are or have been no other proceedings in any court in England and Wales or elsewhere with reference to the marriage (or to any child of the family) or between the petitioner and respondent with reference to any property of either or both of them _except_

Section 7

There are or have been no other proceedings in any court in England and Wales or elsewhere with reference to the marriage (or to any child of the family) or between the Petitioner and Respondent with reference to any property of either or both of them **except** ....

If there have not been any court proceedings in England and Wales concerning:

- ○ your marriage;
- ○ any child of the family; or
- ○ any property belonging to you or your **spouse**,

cross out *except*.

If there have been other proceedings (such as an abortive **divorce petition** in a different court), you need to leave *except* and fill in:

- ○ the name of the court in which the proceedings took place;
- ○ details of any court orders which were made; and
- ○ if the proceedings were about your marriage, whether you and your **spouse** resumed living together as husband and wife after the order was made.

They might or might not affect your current proceedings. It is sensible to seek legal advice.

> (8) There are or have been no proceedings in the Child Support Agency with reference to the maintenance of any child of the family _except_

Section 8

There are or have been no proceedings in the Child Support Agency with reference to the maintenance of any child of the family **except** ....

This one came in with the Child Support Act in 1993. If you have had no dealings with the **Child Support Agency (CSA)**, cross out *except*.

If there have been any proceedings, give:

o   the date of any application to the CSA;

o   details of the assessment that was made.

> (9)   There are no proceedings continuing in any country outside England or Wales which are in respect of the marriage or are capable of affecting its validity or subsistence *except*

Section 9

*There are no proceedings continuing in any country outside England and Wales, which are in respect of thr marriage or are capable of affecting its validity or subsistence **except** ....*

This deals with proceedings abroad. If this means you, you need legal advice.

If there have been no proceedings in a court outside England and Wales which have affected the marriage, or might possibly affect it, cross out *except*.

If there are or have been proceedings, give:

o   the name of the country and the court in which they are taking or have taken place;

o   details of the orders made; or

o   if no order has yet been made, the date of any future hearing.

> (10)   (This paragraph should be completed only if the petition is based on five years' separation.)
> No agreement or arrangement has been made or is proposed to be made between the parties for the support of the petitioner/respondent (and any child of the family) *except*

Section 10

*(This paragraph should be completed only if the **petition** is based on five years' separation.)*

You are going for '**behaviour**' here. Write 'Not applicable' below and go on to section 11.

| (11) | The said marriage has broken down irretrievably. |

Section 11

The said marriage has broken down irretrievably.

Do not write anything.

The Respondent has behaved in such a way that the Petitioner cannot reasonably be expected to live with the Respondent.

Do not write anything.

(12)

Section 12

They have left this blank. This is so that *you* can insert one of five paragraphs which they give in their 'Notes for Guidance' (see p 73). For a **'behaviour' petition** you need their paragraph (b).

Write: 'The Respondent has behaved in such a way that the Petitioner cannot reasonably be expected to live with the Respondent.'

(13)	**Particulars**

Section 13

Here there is a space for the 'particulars' of your **spouse's** behaviour. Your mantra should be 'The **Respondent** has behaved in such a way that the **Petitioner** cannot reasonably be expected to live with the Respondent'.

The **petition** should not contain a paperback book listing all your spouse's bad habits, nor should it include a full history of your arguments and unpleasant incidents. However, you do need to ensure that the particulars contain sufficient detail to satisfy the court that your spouse has behaved unreasonably and has done so quite recently. Bear in mind that what *you* regard as unreasonable in the extreme might not impress the judge at all.

Turn to Chapter 20, 'Some real life "behaviour" particulars', for suggestions. Always finish with: 'Both parties are agreed that the marriage is at an end.' Then, even if the judge thinks your spouse's behaviour was not particularly objectionable, they will heave a deep sigh and agree to the **divorce**.

Prayer

The petitioner therefore prays

(1) **The suit**

   That the said marriage be dissolved

(2) **Costs**

   That the   may be ordered to pay the costs of this suit

(3) **Ancillary relief**

   That the petitioner may be granted the following ancillary relief:

   (a)   an order for maintenance pending suit

         a periodical payments order

         a secured provision order

         a lump sum order

         a property adjustment order

         an order under section 24B, 25B or 25C of the Act of 1973 (Pension Sharing/Attachment Order)

   (b)   **For the children**

         a periodical payments order

         a secured provision order

         a lump sum order

         a property adjustment order

                                                   Signed

Prayer

Not a plea for God to give you strength to get all this form-filling right first time, but an appeal to the court to grant you:

o   a **divorce**;

o   your costs; and

o   **ancillary relief**

   –   for you and

   –   for the children.

Leave all this untouched, even if at this stage you do not want your **spouse** to pay your costs or to pay maintenance, etc. A wise old family lawyer once said, 'They're easier to strike out than put in'. The matter in hand is your divorce; you will argue over the financial details later.

Signed

Do not forget to sign!

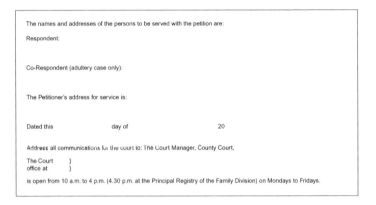

The names and addresses of the persons to be served with the petition are:

Respondent:

Co-Respondent (adultery case only):

The Petitioner's address for service is:

Dated this   day of   20

Address all communications for the court to: The Court Manager, County Court,

The Court   }
office at   }

is open from 10 a.m. to 4 p.m. (4.30 p.m. at the Principal Registry of the Family Division) on Mondays to Fridays.

The names and addresses of the persons to be served with this petition are:

Fill in:

ɔ   your **spouse's** name and address;

ɔ   your address (*address for service* just means the address the court is to send communications to);

ɔ   date;

ɔ   the address of your local **county court**.

In the

*Delete as
appropriate

County Court*

No.

In the Principal Registry*

Between

Petitioner

and

Respondent

Divorce Petition

Full name and address of the petitioner or
of solicitors if they are acting for the petitioner.

Now fill in the front sheet.

You may find it confusing that the front sheet actually goes back to front at the back of the document. This is so that when the document is folded vertically all the details are immediately visible.

'Adultery' petition

This is a straightforward form to fill in. Everything is as in the **'behaviour'** **petition**, above, until you get to section 12. But before you fill the form in, ask yourself:

ɔ Have you and your **spouse** lived together for more than six months after you found out about their adultery?

   If so, a straightforward adultery petition is no longer open to you. All is not lost, however – use 'Behaviour' instead.

ɔ Do you wish to name the **Co-respondent** (your spouse's lover)?

   There is no requirement for you to do so. In fact, in some situations you might not even know the other man/woman's name! Section 12 of the form gives you the choice.

If you feel strongly about it, however, you can certainly name the Co-respondent, but be absolutely sure of your facts before you do so. Also think hard before you do this if you want to avoid inflaming the situation. It might cost you dearly. If vengeance is more important to you than an amicable personal and financial settlement, then by all means name and shame! In that case, the **divorce** petition will be served on the Co-respondent as well as on the **Respondent**, which could contribute to a second marriage breakdown.

If there is any doubt about getting your **spouse** to admit to adultery, or if you are at all hazy about dates and/or whodunit, opt for **'Behaviour'** instead!

Now fill in the form exactly as in the 'Behaviour' petition above, except for section 12, where you write either:

ɔ 'The Respondent has committed adultery with a [man] [woman] and the Petitioner finds it intolerable to live with the Respondent.'

Or

ɔ   'The Respondent has committed adultery with
.... [give the name] (called the Co-
respondent) and the Petitioner finds it intolerable to
live with the Respondent.'

Then go on exactly as in the 'behaviour' petition above.

'Two years' separation' petition

You do not need to do anything creative here! Provided
you put the:

ɔ   names;

ɔ   addresses and, most importantly;

ɔ   dates

in the right places, you should be home and dry.

Interlude: what's meant by 'separation'?

Preferably you should have been living under separate
rooves throughout the two years. Otherwise this is a
difficult one to prove, though not impossible (see 'Under
one roof?', p 9).

What about periods of reconciliation, during which you
got back together? A brief get-together would not count,
but if you get together for a month or more you may
have to add that time to the two years. Separation
involves a withdrawal from married life.

If you decide to have another – or more than one –
attempt at married life together during your separation
but the attempt(s) fail(s), this will not prevent you from
taking the previous period(s) of separation into account
when totting up the two years' separation, *provided* that
the period or periods during which you got back
together *did not exceed six months in total*. Brief periods of
resumption of married life are disregarded by the court
if they are less than, or in total, six months only. Longer
periods might disqualify you altogether or, depending
upon the history of your relationship, may mean that
you have to wait for a longer time before you can apply

for a **divorce** based upon two years' separation with consent. You may be able to rely on part of the period you were separated, but because of a reconciliation you may have effectively postponed the date when you can apply for your divorce.

Take, as an example, Paul and Polly, who separated in November 2001 but got together again in January 2002 for eight months before separating for good in September 2002. Although Paul and Polly initially separated in November 2001, they could not apply for a divorce based on two years' separation in November 2003 because they lived together for too long in 2002. Their period of separation only started to run again in September 2002. If, however, they stay separated until September 2004, they will then be able to rely on two years' separation in order to obtain their divorce.

Molly and Mike, on the other hand, separated in August 2002 and lived together in October for two weeks before separating again. In November 2002 they had another try at living together, which fell apart before Christmas 2002. The *total* period they have lived together during their separation is *less than six months* and they can apply for their divorce in August 2004, that is, as soon as they have been separated for two years. Molly and Mike's brief times back together do not mean that they have to start the period of two years' separation all over again in the way Paul and Polly had to do in September 2002.

Now fill in the form exactly as for the '**behaviour**' **petition** above, until you come to section 12. Here you write: 'The parties to the marriage have lived apart for a continuous period of at least two years immediately preceding the presentation of the petition and the Respondent consents to a divorce being granted.'

Then go on exactly as in the 'behaviour' petition.

'Five years' separation' petition

Fill in exactly as for the **'behaviour'** petition, until you get to section 10.

Section 10

No agreement or arrangement has been made or is proposed to be made between the parties for the support of the Petitioner/Respondent (and any child of the family) except ...

If no agreement or arrangement has been made, cross out *except*.

If an agreement or arrangement has been made between you:

ɔ   about maintenance for either of you or for any child of the family; or

ɔ   about the family property,

give full details.

Section 11

Do not write anything.

Section 12

You need to write: 'The parties to the marriage have lived apart for a continuous period of at least five years immediately preceding the presentation of the petition.'

Then carry on as for the 'behaviour' petition.

Filling in the Statement of Arrangements for Children

What is a child?

For the purposes of the **divorce petition**, this means:

o   all the **Petitioner**'s children;

o   all the **Respondent**'s children; and

o   any children the pair of them have adopted,

whatever their ages. You have to list them all in your petition, together with their dates of birth. If they are over 18 you should say so.

For the purposes of the **Statement of Arrangements for Children**, however, grown-up children do not count.

The Statement of Arrangements must include any child who was born to you and the Respondent, or who has been treated by you as one of the family, who is either:

o   under 16; or

o   between 16 and 18 and still at school or college full-time.

This includes children who were born to *either* of you by previous relationships and whom you have *both* adopted, but *not* foster children.

What sort of arrangements do you have to make? In the eyes of the court, the needs of the children come first. You too must put them first.

All this is set out on a court form, form D8A, the Statement of Arrangements for Children (you will find a copy on p 139). You will have to fill in:

o   the names and dates of birth of the children involved;

o   who they live with and where, and whether this will be different after the divorce;

o   arrangements for their day-to-day care;

o   their health;

o   where they will go to school;

o   what financial support they will receive;

o   contact arrangements (visiting rights) between the children and the **non-resident parent**;

o   any special needs the children may have;

o   any care or court proceedings.

The court does not need to make an order about all the things contained in the Statement of Arrangements for Children, provided the arrangements are in the children's best interests. In fact, the court would prefer it if you could deal with these matters amicably yourselves. If you have agreed the arrangements, you can get your **spouse** to sign the form before you send your various papers to the court. Otherwise, the court will send a copy of your signed Statement of Arrangements for Children to your spouse asking them to confirm whether or not they agree with the arrangements you are proposing.

If the court is not happy with the arrangements, it can make an order (known as 'exercising its powers under the Children Act 1989') changing the arrangements. Mostly, however, courts feel that it is better if the parents (and the children too, if they are old enough) can agree these things together. They are right. You and your spouse really *must* co-operate on this matter if you want your divorce to go smoothly.

You may need to agree arrangements on other child-related topics that may not appear in the Statement of Arrangements. Examples are:

o   arrangements for contact with grandparents and other relations;

o   school fees;

o   clubs and societies.

Not in agreement?

Let us suppose, however, that you and your **spouse** are at loggerheads over the children. What will happen then? Well, the judge might decide to hold up your **divorce** proceedings until you are able to agree on satisfactory arrangements for the children. Then, if you are still at odds, the judge has several options, including:

ɔ   asking you both for further information to enable him to make a decision;

ɔ   asking you both to come and discuss the problem. This will normally be 'in chambers' – in the judge's private room, with only you, your spouse and the judge present;

ɔ   referring you and your spouse to a **mediator**, usually a Court Welfare Officer.

When the judge is satisfied that the children will be properly cared for, they will issue a certificate known as a D84B. This form makes it clear that the court has decided not to exercise its powers under the Children Act 1989. In open-and-shut cases, this certificate is issued as a matter of course. If there have been disagreements, the certificate shows the world that the disputes have been resolved and that the court is no longer anxious about the children.

If you are the Respondent

In **divorce** proceedings the **Petitioner** makes all the running, pays the court fees (though they may claim them back from the **Respondent**) and does the lion's share of the form-filling.

We hope that the divorce **petition** does not come to you out of a clear blue sky. In an ideal world you and your **spouse** will have discussed arrangements for any children in advance, and possibly even have agreed on which 'fact' (see p 7) to use in the petition. However, rather than take such things for granted, the guide below assumes that you have *not* agreed anything in advance.

Your path through the maze

1 Petition arrives

Enclosed with it:

- **Acknowledgment of Service**;
- Notice of Proceedings together with Notes on Questions in the Acknowledgment of Service;
- **Statement of Arrangements for Children** (if children are involved).

Action:

- Read the **petition** carefully.
- Read the Statement of Arrangements for Children carefully and check to make sure all the information (for example, dates of birth, etc) is accurate and that you agree with the proposals for the children.

If you agree, sign and date it.

o   Read Notice of Proceedings and Notes on Questions in the Acknowledgment of Service carefully.

o   Complete and sign Acknowledgment of Service.

o   Return Acknowledgment of Service and Statement of Arrangements (if applicable) to court within seven days.

2 Certificate of Entitlement to a Decree arrives

Action: None, there is no need to go to court on the date fixed for pronouncement of the **Decree Nisi**.

3 Decree Nisi arrives

Action: None

4 Decree Absolute arrives

Action: Put it in a safe place.

Now make your will and notify the Inland Revenue and National Insurance office of your change in status from a married to a single person.

A note on form-filling

There are different Acknowledgment of Service forms for all occasions (well, Adultery and Behaviour share one, but it is quite straightforward). Have no fear! The court will send you the right form for your situation, together with the correct Notice of Proceedings and Notes on Questions in the Acknowledgment of Service.

With the Acknowledgment of Service you will receive a Notice of Proceedings, including Notes on Questions in the Acknowledgment of Service. You have seven days to sign and return your paperwork to the court.

This might be a convenient time to remind you that forms were created for a reason: to obtain and set out information in a form (sorry, no pun intended) convenient for the people who process them for a living.

Many people complain bitterly that what they want to say never seems to fit into the various boxes on a standard form, or that they find the questions ambiguous or even incomprehensible. We sympathise. However, Rosy recalls the time when she was a young Open Competition Civil Servant in the mid-1960s. She found herself struggling to write a policy document based on information that local authorities had submitted in wildly differing formats. Despite being a founder member of Form Phobics Anonymous, Rosy ended up devising a form to pluck information from the various submissions, collate that information and present it in an easily accessible manner. That, in essence, is why we have to have forms: to present information in an easily accessible manner.

We've made this point before, but it's worth saying twice: cultivate a court clerk. They are all superb form-fillers. Most seem to have been selected for their neat, legible handwriting and willingness to help. They will take in their stride things that throw form phobics, such as the little matter of the numbers in the Notes on Questions in the **Acknowledgment of Service** not corresponding with the numbers of the questions in the Acknowledgment of Service form itself.

Question I

1   Write 'Yes' (unless they forgot to enclose the petition!).

1A If, as is usually the case, there are no other court proceedings (such as any earlier attempts at **divorce**) involving your marriage, write 'No'.

If there *are* other court proceedings, then you need to write full details in the form and attach copies of any relevant documents. You may also need to consult a solicitor in case there is unfinished business to clear up before continuing with the present **divorce** proceedings.

1B Put *either* England *or* Wales if you have always lived in either (or indeed both) of these countries. Otherwise, this question is concerned with your *domicile* – that is, the country that you treat as your permanent home and to which you have the closest legal ties (see p 74 for a fuller explanation of this).

If you are in any doubt about this section, seek professional advice.

1C Asks if you agree with your **spouse** that the court has **jurisdiction** in this case.

If you are in any doubt, seek professional advice.

Question 2

Write the date the **petition** was delivered to you and the address where you received it. Normally this would be your home address, but if the petition was handed to you somewhere else (such as at your work address), put that address.

Question 3

Write 'Yes' (unless there has been some dreadful mistake and the **petition** is not intended for you at all!).

Question 4

Write 'No'.

In 15 years of family law practice, Jane has come across two fully **defended divorces**, as opposed to **answers** and **cross-petitions**. Defending divorce proceedings is *not* a DIY matter. If you do plan to defend, or even to send an answer, seek professional advice at once.

Question 5 onwards

Then the forms diverge and the numbering is different for each version. For example, in adultery proceedings Question 5 asks if you admit to committing adultery, whereas in two years' separation matters Question 5 is 'Do you consent to a decree being granted?' and in five years' separation proceedings it is 'Do you intend to oppose the grant of a decree on the grounds that the divorce will result in grave financial or other hardship to you and that in all the circumstances it would be wrong to dissolve the marriage?'

Read your Notes on Questions carefully before answering each question. They are quite user-friendly, but here are some points to remember:

o   Adultery: If you do not admit that you have committed adultery, seek professional advice at once.

o   Behaviour: If you do not agree that you have behaved unreasonably, seek professional advice at once.

o   Two years' separation: If you do not agree to a divorce, seek professional advice at once.

o   Five years' separation: If you intend to defend because a divorce will cause you grave financial hardship, or if you think it would be wrong to dissolve the marriage, write 'Yes' – and seek professional advice at once.

o   You will be asked (the question number varies according to the type or petition) whether you object to paying the costs of the proceedings. You can object if you wish, but you are unlikely to be successful in avoiding altogether unless the **Petitioner** is getting **Legal Help**, or is doing the **divorce** as a **litigant in person** without professional legal advice.

Sometimes it is possible to agree to split the costs with the Petitioner so that you only pay an agreed share. If you reach an agreement about costs, say so in your reply, setting out the amount you have agreed to pay. If your **spouse** is legally represented, make sure your agreement clarifies whether or not your contribution includes VAT.

○ Two years' and five years' separation: You are asked whether you want the court to decide on financial matters for you. If you are uncertain, write 'Yes, if financial matters cannot be agreed by consent'. In other words, you have not at the time of filling in this form agreed a financial settlement and you are keeping your options open in case negotiations between you and your spouse break down.

○ Statement of Arrangements for Children: If there is one, read it carefully before answering those questions. Check the date next to the Petitioner's signature and enter the relevant date in the Acknowledgment of Service form.

If you disagree, seek professional legal advice immediately and before you return the **Acknowledgment of Service** or the Statement of Arrangements to the court. In some cases where there has been a factual mistake (such as giving the wrong date of birth for one of the children, or the child has changed schools), you may be able insert a reply simply correcting the factual error. For example, 'Our son David's date of birth is the 1/02/1999, not 2/03/98 as stated by the **Petitioner**. In all other respects, I agree with the Statement of Arrangements'.

○ Polygamous marriages: If this applies to you, seek professional advice.

Final paragraph

Are you a litigant in person? If so, sign and date at (a).

If you have a solicitor acting for you, they will sign at (b) on your behalf. However, if you are admitting adultery, or if you are objecting to paying costs, you will need to sign and date the first section too.

The next stages

See our diagram on p 65. If you are the **Petitioner**, the court **serves** a copy of your **petition** and **Statement of Arrangements for Children** on your **spouse**. They now have seven days – starting from the day after the petition drops on their doormat – to respond. If you have **filed** an adultery petition and there is a **Co-respondent**, they get a copy of the petition too.

If you are the Petitioner, at the same time the court sends you a **Notice of Issue of Petition and Postal Service** which tells you when the petition was sent out. It will also give you your case number, which you must write on the front of your file in thick black felt tip – you will need it!

Acknowledgment of Service

An **Acknowledgment of Service** is confirmation to the court that the **petition** was **served** on (that is, sent to) you. The **Respondent** has to file this Acknowledgment of Service and, if your **spouse** has not signed it beforehand, the **Statement of Arrangements for Children** if children are involved – with the court within (their words) '7 days after you receive this notice', although the court will usually allow some extra time, especially if the Respondent lives abroad.

What if the Respondent does not return the papers? You can ask the court to instruct their bailiff, and we show you how to do this (see the sample covering letter, p 159). It may well, however, be more effective to instruct a process server (see 'Power point', p 63).

It is, of course, sensible to make sure that your spouse will co-operate before starting proceedings.

Directions for Trial

Once your **spouse** has returned the papers, the court will send you a photocopy of the **Acknowledgment of Service** together with an **Application for Directions for Trial**. We have included a sample on p 150.

Generals give orders. Judges give directions. An **Application for Directions for Trial** is not demanding a courtroom battle but is merely a formal request for your **divorce** proceedings to go on to the next stage.

With the Application is an **affidavit**, a questionnaire which you have to complete before **swearing** or affirming (see p xx) that everything is true. This questionnaire will vary depending on which kind of **divorce** you are applying for – the separation one is different from the adultery one, for example. The court will (one hopes) send you the correct form, although they have been known to get this wrong, so do check for yourself.

Don't be hasty!

1   Check on the Acknowledgment of Service the date when the **Respondent** says they received the **petition**. You cannot apply for directions for trial until *nine days* after that date.

2   Check that the Respondent has actually signed the Acknowledgment of Service – you will have to swear that this is their signature.

3   The affidavit has to be sworn and witnessed, so don't sign it until the person witnessing it tells you to do so.

4   Swearing or affirming an affidavit will cost you about £7 if you swear or affirm it in front of a solicitor (if you are on **Legal Help**, keep the receipt and claim the money back through your solicitor). If you swear or affirm before an officer of the court, there is no charge.

Swearing or affirming is not a trivial matter. You will need to swear on the Bible (or Qu'ran if you are Muslim) that the contents of your form are true. *If you have any doubts, don't swear.*

Now photocopy everything. Put your photocopies in your divorce file and and send to the court:

o   Application for Directions for Trial;

o   affidavit;

o   covering letter (see p 158).

Certificate of Entitlement

If you have got your paperwork right, you and your **spouse** will each receive a rather unimpressive piece of paper headed **Certificate of Entitlement to a Decree** (see p 148). It will say that the judge agrees you are entitled to a **divorce**, and will give a date on which the **Decree Nisi** will be pronounced.

If you receive anything other than a Certificate of Entitlement, it probably means you made a mistake with your form-filling. Check your paperwork again, or consider ringing the court and asking where you went wrong.

Decree Nisi

Check the date, and mark in your diary the date six weeks and one day after the **Decree Nisi**. That is the date on which you can apply for the **decree** to be made absolute. Your **spouse** will receive a Decree Nisi too.

Nisi is Latin for `unless`. And *unless* the couple decide not to go through with the **divorce** (which has been known to happen both in fiction and in real life), the next step will be the real thing – the **Decree Absolute**.

You may be in a tearing hurry to apply for your **decree** to be made absolute, but if there is money and/or property at stake *you must not be hasty.* Here are two very good reasons for holding back your application.

1   If the family home is in your spouse's sole name and you want to protect your **matrimonial home rights**, you should be aware that a **Decree Absolute** will normally end your right to live in the family home (see Chapter 17 for details).

2   If you are claiming **ancillary relief** of any kind, this needs to be sorted out before your **divorce** is made final. If you steam ahead and get your Decree Absolute without finalising these matters, you could lose everything. As always where money and property are at stake, you must take professional advice.

Decree Absolute

On DA Day, fill in the application form for decree to be made absolute (see a copy on the companion website) and send it to the court with a cheque for £30 payable to Her Majesty's Paymaster General and the covering letter on p 164. (Of course, if you are publicly funded you get this service free of charge.)

You and your ex should each receive a **Decree Absolute**. See the sample on p 155. You can now hold a mild celebration. You did it all by yourself, you saved at least £700 in legal fees and hopefully you and your ex are still speaking.

Now keep your Decree Absolute certificate in a very safe place. Also, if you have not already done so – make your will.

Make your will!

Divorce affects any will you may have made before. It is always wise to make a will, and especially wise if you and your **spouse** are at odds. If you delay in making your will and the unthinkable happens, your spouse may get everything and someone you love may lose out. We remember a 29-year-old mother of three who died suddenly during divorce proceedings. We had sent her a draft will, but she had not yet signed it. Her drunken, violent husband got the lot.

You need *Living Wills and Enduring Powers of Attorney* in the *Pocket Lawyer* series to ensure that if the unthinkable happens, your money and property will go to the right people – and that any children will be cared for by the person of your choice. Otherwise your ex-spouse, as the surviving parent, will automatically have sole care of the children. If you wish someone else to be responsible for the children after your death, you need to appoint a guardian or guardians in your will. They will normally act jointly with your surviving spouse. This assumes that your spouse is the parent of, or has parental responsibility for, your children. You may be eligible for **Legal Help** to cover the cost of preparing a will to appoint guardian(s) for your children where you are estranged, separated, or divorcing their other parent.

Jointly owned property

Wills are especially important if you own a house jointly with your **spouse** (see Chapter 17). This is because, if the two of you own your home as *joint tenants* (which is usually the case), the other joint tenant will inherit your share of the property when you die. Suppose you died in the middle of divorcing the other joint tenant for adultery. Would you want your soon-to-be-ex, rather than your children, to inherit your share?

'Tenant' here has nothing to do with being a tenant in the sense of paying rent to a landlord. 'Tenant' in this context comes from the Latin for 'have or hold' (in this case, some property).

You can change this situation by severing the joint tenancy so that you and your spouse become *tenants in common*. This sounds difficult, but is in fact very easy; we have included a standard document on p 119 to enable you to do this. **Do remember to send it to your spouse – it doesn't work unless you do this!**

A similar situation arises if the two of you have joint insurance policies.

It is difficult to generalise; you would have to consult your individual insurer.

Dividing the spoils

Getting divorced is usually fairly simple. It is **ancillary relief** – the money and property side of **divorce** – that takes up the most time and causes the most trouble. You and your **spouse** will need to draw up a list of what you own and what you owe.

Take advantage of all the free advice you can get. Most banks and building societies are helpful. Always tell them exactly what you are up to: why, for example, you are closing the joint account or making a new standing order. They may be able to suggest something you had not even thought of.

A note on Consent Orders

Even if you have handled your **divorce** proceedings yourself – and saved at least £700 in legal fees – you would be wise to instruct a solicitor to make sure the financial side of your divorce is legally sound as well as fair to both you and your **spouse**. Even if you are both penniless now, who's to know whether one of you will come into money and find your ex demanding their share? Far better, surely, to tie up all the loose ends.

Perhaps the best way of doing this is to get your solicitor to draft a **Consent Order** to be 'blessed' by the judge. The usual time to do this is between the **Decree Nisi** and the **Decree Absolute**. At the time of writing, the court will not even look at a draft Consent Order before the Decree Nisi stage.

A Consent Order is legally binding. It tidies up technical but potentially important matters such as excluding claims under the Inheritance Act and the Married

Women's Property Act. The order closes doors which would otherwise be left wide open to potential claims – see below.

The Married Women's Property Act 1882 was a major milestone in women's rights. Before 1882, a wife's property belonged to her husband. Today, unless her rights under the Act are specifically excluded, an ex-wife will continue to have statutory rights against her ex-husband.

Guidelines for ancillary relief

It is not the purpose of this book to cover **ancillary relief** in any detail. We believe that if property and money are at stake, you need to call in the professionals to advise on your individual case, rather than relying on general advice in a paperback book!

It is, however, important for you to know the points a court would look at in making any financial settlement.

Guidelines

One of the courts' key guidelines is a list of factors set out in section 25 of the Matrimonial Causes Act 1973. It makes stodgy reading, but it is important and you should take it on board. The same guidelines would be used for Mr and Mrs Average and the Duke and Duchess of York. The court must consider, for each of you:

o   present income;
o   present and future earning capacity;
o   property and other financial resources;
o   financial needs, responsibilities and obligations, present and future;
o   the family's standard of living before the marriage broke down;
o   the age of each of you;
o   how long you have been married;

- whether either of you suffers from any disability, either mental or physical;
- how much and/or in what way each of you has contributed to the welfare of the family (this covers more than breadwinning; it also takes into account looking after the home or caring for the family);
- in certain situations, how each of you has behaved;
- lost opportunities – the value of any benefit which either of you will lose the chance of if you divorce (this would, for example, apply to pension rights).

Many financial settlements are reached without going to court except to get a **Consent Order** 'blessed' by the judge, but the lawyers who brokered these amicable settlements would have taken all these points into consideration. They would be aware, for example, that the court will not only consider any benefits under a pension scheme which either **spouse** is likely to have, but would also take note of any benefits you or your spouse might have otherwise enjoyed if you had not **divorced**.

The Matrimonial Causes Act headings provide the court with a starting point only and the Court still has complete discretion to make such orders for **ancillary relief** as it thinks fit in all the circumstances.

Children

The court follows similar statutory guidelines when making decisions about financial provision for the child(ren) of the family.

These include:

- the financial needs of the child(ren) of the family;
- the financial resources of the child(ren), including their income and/or earning capacity;
- any physical or mental disability of the child(ren);
- the way in which the child(ren) is/are being educated or trained and the way in which you both expected them to be educated or trained;
- the matters set out in the 'grown-up' guidelines, above.

We cannot stress sufficiently the advantages of reaching a financial agreement that you can then ask the court to bless in the form of a **Consent Order**. The court fee for a Consent Order is £30. Getting a solicitor to draw one up to your requirements will cost a great deal less than slugging it out in the court, especially if you do your homework first.

Some financial considerations

We told you – splitting up is simple if you are homeless, penniless or childless. Everyone else has all manner of financial loose ends to tie up. Here are a few.

National Insurance (NI)

Wives may have been paying the reduced rate NI contributions (the 'married woman's stamp'). If this applies to you, you *must* tell your employer as soon as your **Decree Absolute** comes through (or, in the case of a **judicial separation**, your Decree of Judicial Separation). You must then ask your employer to help you to inform the National Insurance Office that you are no longer married. This, not surprisingly, requires you to fill in a special form, but your employer should have one in stock. You (or hopefully your employer) will then need to send the form to the Inland Revenue National Insurance Contributions Office (see 'Useful contacts', p 165).

If you do not tell the National Insurance Office about your change of status, you can be held personally responsible for any underpayment which could affect your future entitlement to benefits and state pension.

If you are self-employed at the time of your **Decree Absolute**, you will become liable to pay Class 2 contributions from the date your Decree came through. You must let the National Insurance Office know by completing a special form, which you can get from your nearest branch of the Department for Work and Pensions (DWP) (formerly DSS) or Inland Revenue.

Civil servants in the DWP and the Inland Revenue, like court clerks, are ace form-fillers. If form-filling isn't your forte, go down to your nearest office and throw yourself on their mercy.

You must then send the completed form to the Inland Revenue National Insurance Contributions Office (see 'Useful contacts', p 165).

Benefits

If your Decree Absolute came through before you reached state pension age, you may still be able to get incapacity benefit (provided you are incapacitated, of course) and job seeker's allowance if you have enough contributions and credits in your own right.

If a woman remarries before reaching state pension age, she cannot use her previous **spouse's** contributions to help her to get a retirement pension. Her retirement pension will instead be based on her and her new husband's National Insurance contribution records.

If you are a woman and your marriage ends before you reach state pension age, you may still be entitled to incapacity benefit and job seeker's allowance but these will be less than if you claimed retirement pension, so when you reach 65 you should claim retirement pension instead. This is split into two parts – the basic pension, which is a flat rate, and the additional pension, which is earnings related. You can use your ex-husband's contribution record to help you to get a basic retirement pension if his contribution record is better than yours.

More about benefits

When you separate or **divorce** you may need to consider claiming state benefits instead of any income you previously received from your former **spouse**. You may be entitled to *job seeker's allowance* if you are able to work but are not working, or are working on average 16 hours or less per week. If you have children, you may also be entitled to *child benefit*. People are entitled to *income support* if they are:

ɔ   over 16 years old;

ɔ   on a low income;

ɔ   have savings under a certain amount (usually a maximum of £8,000 but not always);

o   not working; *or*

o   working fewer than 16 hours per week.

A new system for family support started in April 2003. It is called *child tax credit* and *working tax credit.*

Child tax credit replaces allowances given for children previously incorporated within income support, working family tax credit, job seeker's allowance, the former children's tax credit and disabled person's tax credit. Under the Tax Credits Act 2002, child tax credit is now available to persons who are responsible for at least one child or a 'qualifying young person' – for example, an individual under the age of 19 and still in full-time education, but not advanced education such as university. Child tax credit is also available in respect of a young person who has not yet reached the age of 18 but who has registered for work or training and has not been in full-time education for a consecutive period of 20 weeks.

Working tax credit is available to people aged 16 or over in paid employment for fewer than 16 hours per week and who are responsible for at least one child, or are disabled, or those who are aged 25 or over and normally work for at least 30 hours per week.

There are complex formulas for calculating the amount of child tax credit and working tax credit, but if you think you may be eligible for either or both of these tax credits you can obtain more details and order application forms from the Inland Revenue website (see 'Useful contacts', p 164).

Anyone who is on a low income and paying rent can claim *housing benefit,* and they can claim *Council Tax benefit* whether they are paying rent or not.

Of course, if you have children and their other parent is living elsewhere you can claim *child support* from the **Child Support Agency (CSA)**. It is more common for mothers to claim, but fathers can too.

Pensions for people divorcing

If you **divorce** or get a **decree** of **judicial separation**, any financial settlement or maintenance payments can be affected by the value of any pension you and your **spouse** may have paid into. The court can order that most of this pension should be shared between you, even if it is in only one spouse's name.

Note that if you separate (other than judicially – see above) but do not divorce, pensions cannot be shared in this way.

17

The family home: safeguarding your rights

'Matrimonial home' is law-speak for the family home. Both **spouses** have the right to live there. These rights used to be called 'rights of occupation' (law-speak for the right to live in a property) and many lawyers still use that term, but the buzzword today is **matrimonial home rights**.

If you are considering a **divorce**, you should think about whether you need to protect your right to live in the family home as a precautionary measure. Long term decisions – such as who will live in the family home after the divorce and how the proceeds will be shared if it is sold – will have to be made as part of the financial side of the divorce. In the meantime, you need to safeguard your right to live there.

A spouse who does not legally own the family home – that is, whose name is not on the title deeds – still has certain rights:

o   the right not to be evicted without a court order if they are actually living there;

o   the right (if the court so decides) to return to the family home if they have left it;

o   the right (if the court so decides) temporarily to exclude either spouse from the family home, even if the property is in their name. This does not usually happen except in cases of domestic violence (see Chapter 8).

Rented homes

The same principle applies to rented homes such as council or housing association property. Even if the tenancy agreement is in the sole name of one **spouse** (let's say Paul), his wife Polly will have **matrimonial home rights** until the fate of the family home has been decided, usually at the end of **divorce** proceedings.

Note that if Paul moves out and Polly intends to stay put, Polly must take steps to have the tenancy transferred into her name *as soon as possible and, in any event, before the divorce is made absolute.* This is because, by staying in the family home, she is keeping the tenancy alive under the 'deemed occupation' rules of the Matrimonial Homes Act 1983. Recent case law shows, however, that Paul might be able to get Polly out anyway – see below.

There have been cases where the sole tenant has served notice on the landlord – usually a local authority – to terminate the tenancy if they believe they will have to move out leaving their **spouse** in the property. This is a spiteful thing to do, but unless the spouse left in the property has written to the landlord asking to be told about any such notice, this despicable tactic may work. Just writing to the landlord may also in itself be insufficient protection. *The best thing is to get the tenancy transferred straight away* and we would suggest you get professional advice. Remember that if you are receiving benefits, you can instruct a solicitor under the **Legal Help Scheme**.

'Owned' homes

Let us suppose Paul and Polly own their own home jointly. For the purposes of **matrimonial home rights**, it does not matter whether or not they have a mortgage. Neither of them needs to register their matrimonial home rights. This is because neither **spouse** will be able to sell or mortgage the property without the other's knowledge, because both names would show up if a potential buyer or lender carried out a search of the property title.

If the family home is in one spouse's sole name, it's a different story.

In one spouse's sole name

Suppose the family home is owned by Paul in his sole name. Polly still has matrimonial home rights:

o   Paul cannot exclude her, or legally evict her, from the family home; *and*

o   Polly can make sure Paul does not sell the house without her permission.

The same would apply if Polly was the sole owner: the rules are unisex. We first mentioned this briefly in 'Protecting the family home' on p 27. Now here is a more detailed explanation.

As long as Polly continues to live in the family home, with or without Paul, she has a legal right under the Matrimonial Homes Act 1983 to stay there until the court orders otherwise, or grants a **Decree Absolute** in her **divorce**. Until then, Paul cannot make her leave the family home, *provided* that:

o   she was living there with Paul while she was married to him; *and*

o   she continued to live there without interruption, despite the breakdown of her marriage.

Polly needs to stay put because she will lose her rights if she moves out of the family home. Even if she only moves out for a short time, she risks losing her matrimonial home rights.

If you think *you* may be entitled to **matrimonial home rights**, but are not sure because you have spent some time away from the family home, seek legal advice immediately.

For example, a very short time – say a week – away from home will probably not affect your rights, especially if you have made it clear to your **spouse** that:

o   you are taking a short break away, whether for a holiday, business purposes or to visit other members of your family; *and*

o   *you are not moving out under any circumstances.*

At the opposite extreme, several months living with someone else with whom you are having a relationship will normally, though not always, lose you your matrimonial home rights.

Enter the Land Registry

So, if your **spouse** is the sole owner of the family home, you need to protect your **matrimonial home rights** by registering a Notice with the Land Registry.

You can register your matrimonial home rights, preventing your spouse from selling or transferring the property to a third party unless they do so with your agreement. Anyone buying the property or lending money on it would carry out what are called 'Land Registry searches' as a matter of course – and find your Notice registering your matrimonial home rights. Even if they failed either to carry out searches at all, or to find your Notice, the fact that you *did* register your matrimonial home rights is enough to protect you. If the house is then sold or mortgaged, this will be done subject to your matrimonial home rights. You can sit tight and the buyer or loan provider cannot turn you out unless you yourself agree to give up your rights!

There are two methods of protecting your rights, depending on whether the legal title to your spouse's property is *registered* or *unregistered* with the Land Registry.

Most homes have their titles (that is, details of who owns them) registered at the Land Registry, because registration of title is now compulsory for the whole of England and Wales. However, there are some areas where registration used to be voluntary, and if your home is in one of these areas and your spouse bought it some years ago, it is possible that the Land Registry has not yet got around to registering it.

Two people who should be able to tell you whether the property is registered are:

o the solicitor who did the legal work when the property was bought;
o if the family home is mortgaged, the mortgage lender.

Other indicators are:

o if there is a mortgage and the bank or building society holds a Land Registry document called a Charge Certificate, then the property is registered;

○ if there is no mortgage and your spouse has a Land Certificate (another Land Registry document), then again the property is registered.

If your investigations come to nothing, you can ask the Land Registry whether the title is registered and, if so, the title number given to the property. Any Citizens Advice Bureau (CAB) should be able to help you to do this – but see 'Power point' below.

---

1   If you are receiving benefits you should be able to instruct a solicitor under the **Legal Help Scheme** to register your **matrimonial home rights**. Even if you do not qualify for Legal Help, a solicitor is unlikely to charge a fortune to do this chore for you. A lot of money is likely to be at stake – do you really want to do this yourself?

2   If you do decide to DIY, your local CAB will be able to guide you through the paperwork.

If the title is registered

Let us suppose you have found that the title is registered. You can now, if you are hellbent on doing this yourself, register your matrimonial home rights. If you have access to the internet, visit the Land Registry website (see 'Useful contacts', p 162) which provides the forms and information you need as well as a helpful leaflet, *Applications Under the Family Law Act 1997 Affecting Registered Land*.

If you do not have access to the internet, you will need to contact either the Land Registry (call the number in 'Useful contacts' and ask for details of your local branch) or your neighbourhood CAB. Either of these will help you to register your matrimonial home rights and of course provide a copy of the leaflet.

If the title is not registered

You can still protect your matrimonial home rights as the non-owning **spouse** by registering a Class F Land Charge at HM Land Charges Department (address is in 'Useful contacts', p 162). At the time of writing, there is no fee for this and your local CAB should be able to help you with the paperwork.

As before, this is something you can have done by a solicitor, either free if you are entitled to **Legal Help** or for a modest fee if you do not qualify, and we do recommend that you instruct one – solicitors carry indemnity insurance and you don't!

Find out if your **spouse** owns a second home.

We are not talking about a cottage in the Dordogne here. Picture this scenario. Polly suspects that Paul has bought another property – he has moved with a new girlfriend, Penny, into a newly bought home which he *says* belongs to Penny.

There is an easy way for Polly to check who legally owns the property, again via the Land Registry. As long as she has the postal address of the new home, the Land Registry will, for a small fee, supply the name and address of the registered owner.

If you follow Polly's example and your suspicions are confirmed – your spouse is shown as a legal owner of a second property – you should take action at once to prevent your spouse from selling or transferring the property without your agreement. Then when you claim **ancillary relief**, the second property will be taken into consideration.

In theory you could do this yourself – it involves yet another Land Registry transaction – but, as always when money and property are at stake, we recommend you seek professional advice.

The effect of registering your **matrimonial home rights** invariably ends once a **decree** of **divorce** is made absolute. But suppose the question of the family home has not been settled by then? You will need to ask the court, before the decree is made absolute, to keep your rights of occupation alive. It is much safer and simpler to delay applying for the **Decree Absolute**. However, if you think your **spouse** will apply for the Decree Absolute, write to the court explaining that you do not want the **Decree Nisi** made absolute for this reason. Then if your spouse applies for the Decree Absolute, the court should notify you of that application. The court usually fixes a hearing to decide whether the Decree Absolute should be made and what steps, if any, should be taken to protect your interest in the **matrimonial** home. Alternatively, if you are making a financial claim for a share of the property you should register a 'pending action' claim, which puts third **parties** on notice of your interest, as discussed above.

We do not think this is a DIY matter, as a great deal of money may be at stake. Please seek professional advice.

Joint ownership and the family home

All the above applies to a family home which is owned *in your spouse's sole name*. Most couples own their homes jointly, either as *beneficial joint tenants* or as *tenants in common*. The main difference between the two is what happens to the property when one of the joint owners dies.

Beneficial joint tenants

If you own the property as *beneficial joint tenants*, the property will pass automatically to the survivor (survivors if more than two people own the property) when one of the joint owners dies.

This arrangement is the usual one between married spouses or cohabitants. The property will pass automatically to the survivor. So, if Paul and Polly are joint tenants:

ɔ   Paul will inherit if Polly dies first; and

ɔ   Polly will inherit if Paul dies first.

This means that while Paul and Polly remain joint beneficial tenants neither can give away, either in their lifetime or in their will when they die, any part of their share in the property. If either of them dies while still owning the property as a joint beneficial tenant, the share of the spouse who has died will automatically pass to the surviving owner.

Tenants in common

If you own the property as *tenants in common*, you will each own a distinct share (usually equal shares, but unequal shares are possible). Because your share is distinct, you can give it away either in your lifetime or in your will. When one tenant in common dies, their share does not automatically go to the survivor. So, if Paul and Polly are tenants in common, *either of them can give away their share in their lifetime or leave it in their will.*

If you are already *beneficial joint tenants* and wish to be *tenants in common*, giving your spouse a simple form of notice will be sufficient to break the beneficial joint tenancy. A sample specimen of a notice, which will turn a joint beneficial tenancy into a tenancy in common, is set out below.

Is the property registered?

Ideally, you should know whether your property has a title number. In other words, has your property been registered at HM Land Registry, or is it still unregistered? Oh dear, we hear you say, this is where I came in! You should be able to find out from:

ɔ   the solicitor who acted for you when you bought your property;

ɔ   your mortgage lender.

If you cannot find out this information do not simply decide not to **serve** the notice on your spouse. Get the title number from the Land Registry (see above).

Now prepare the notice using the specimen sample, below, and give or send it to your spouse.

1   Don't be put off **serving** a **notice** to sever a joint tenancy because you're unable to get the title number. Serve it anyway, rather than not at all.

2   We've said it before and we'll say it again – if you decide to be tenants in common, you must make a will to dispose of your share to other members of your family (see *Living Wills and Enduring Powers of Attorney* in the *Pocket Lawyer* series.

The notice below cancels a *joint tenancy*. You and your spouse will still have equal shares in the family home, but you will be *tenants in common* (see above).

Remember, however, that **serving** a notice severing the joint tenancy could conceivably work against you. Suppose your **spouse** dies before a financial order has been obtained from the court. Once you have served the notice, it will mean that if your spouse dies before you, their interest in the property you previously owned as joint beneficial tenants will no longer automatically pass to you. Sometimes serving a Notice of Severance can be a double-edged sword!

If you are at all doubtful, seek professional advice.

Joint Property – Notice of Severance

From: *[your name and address]*

To: *[co-owner's name and address]*

Property: *[address and Land Registry title number of co-owned property]*

I give you notice that from today the rule of survivorship is not to apply to the above property, and that it is now owned between us as beneficial tenants in common in the following shares:

My share [   ] %

Your share [   ]%

Signed …………………………………………..

Dated …………………………………………..

[on second copy only]

I acknowledge receipt of the original notice, of which this is a copy.

Signed …………………………………………..

Dated …………………………………………..

- Make three copies. Keep one copy for yourself.
- Send your co-owner the original notice plus a copy by recorded delivery, and ask them to confirm that they have received it by dating the copy and putting their signature in the box, which is on the second copy only (see above).
- Your co-owner should then give or send you the second copy back for you to keep.
- Put your copy safely away in the divorce file, which will probably be quite fat by now.

Even if your **spouse** will not sign their copy of the Notice and return it to you, the fact that you sent it by recorded delivery in the post is still sufficient to sever the joint tenancy.

Protecting your interest against third parties

Third parties? Well, yes. Suppose your spouse has borrowed money using the property as security and the lenders are anxious to sell it to get at the money. It happens, unfortunately.

It is not always enough to **serve** a Notice of Severance on your spouse, because although this will change the basis of the ownership of the property, only you and your co-owner will know about the change you have made.

Third parties will not be aware that the two of you have exchanged a Notice of Severance. It may, in some circumstances, be very important to make sure that the change of ownership from beneficial joint tenants to tenants in common becomes public knowledge. If title to the property is registered (see above) and you have obtained details of the title number allocated to your property by the Land Registry, you can tell the world by *registering a restriction*.

Registering a restriction with the Land Registry used to be something you could consider doing yourself, although no one would blame you for getting a professional to do it for you (see below). However, the new Land Registration Act 2002 came into force just days before this book went to press. The Land Registry says: 'The aim of the Act is to simplify improve and modernise land registration law. The Act provides a framework for the development of electronic conveyancing.'

We're sorry, but it doesn't feel like simplification to us, at least not where protecting the family home is concerned. For example, what was once a free service is now likely to cost you £40; and the form required to register a restriction (formerly form 75) is now form AN1, UN1 or RX1, depending on the individual circumstances. You may wish to access the Land Registry website at www.landreg.gov.uk – click on 'Land Registration Act 2002', then on 'Forms and Publications' to see *Fact Sheet 16* which deals with third party interests. For more details, click on 'Practice Guide 19' (notices, restrictions and the protection of third party interests in the register).

At the time of going to press, many professionals, and even Land Registry officials themselves, are still familiarising themselves with the new rules and forms. Fortunately, there is a special Action Line – 0870 908 8061 – to help professionals and lay people alike to get it right.

You will probably take one look at the paperwork involved in this transaction and decide to instruct a solicitor to register the restriction for you. Ask for a quote; it should not cost you a fortune.

It is very much a belt and braces job to make the change in ownership a matter of public record. If you are unable to go the full monty and register a restriction, we strongly recommend that you take the preliminary step of **serving** a Notice of Severance of the joint beneficial ownership on your co-owner(s).

If you are the sole owner of the family home

Stay put!

You do not need to take any further action at this stage; you should simply continue living in your property. But if your **spouse** wishes to stay as well, note (see above) that they have **matrimonial home rights** until the **divorce** is finalised and you cannot, except in certain very limited cases (such as in an incident of domestic violence (see Chapter 8)), insist they move out *earlier*. Even If your spouse leaves the family home, they may still be able to obtain an **occupation order** giving them the right to re-enter your property and live in it again. If you want them to leave and they refuse, seek legal advice before doing anything more.

Managing stress

There are many books about stress on the market, but here are a few notes for starters.

If you press the Thesaurus button on your computer and ask it for a synonym for 'stress', your machine will probably suggest 'pressure, strain, anxiety, constant worry, tension, nervous trauma, hassle'. Anybody who has experienced even the mildest marital disagreement has a first-hand knowledge of stress in all its forms. This is not a book about stress management, but a book about marital breakdown without some reference to the accompanying stress would be like a book on cake making without any oven temperatures.

Which comes first, the breakdown or the stress? Well, stress is responsible for many marriage breakdowns, and any marriage breakdown is guaranteed to generate inordinate amounts of stress. Quite apart from our personal wretchedness and the misery our stress causes other people, stress affects decisions which should be rational and carefully considered.

When we are stressed, our decisions tend to be anything but rational and carefully considered. We are 'not operating on a full deck'; we are 'a few jewels short of a tiara'. We make dodgy decisions, or say unkind and ill-judged things, then wake up in the small hours weeping and sweating and wishing we hadn't. So if you are to save your marriage, or minimise the damage its breakdown does to you, you will need to manage stress.

Normal levels of stress are a necessary and important part of our lives. Without any stress, we would all be brain dead. Stress raises our state of awareness and arousal, improving our performance and making us more alert. Many writers work best under stress. Give them a tight deadline and they fizz with energy. Many family solicitors get a buzz out of emergency proceedings because they are time-critical and the happiness and even safety of a whole family may depend on *their* knowledge, skill, eloquence and perfect paperwork. Perhaps the best example of stress used creatively is on the trading floor of the Stock Exchange.

That sort of stress, in moderation – for we all need a chance to wind down or slob out from time to time – is creative and constructive. However, when the pressure intensifies to a point where the individual feels out of control, stress is harmful and destructive.

Stress can manifest itself in many ways. It can make you lose all confidence and self esteem. It can affect your concentration and make you withdraw into daydreams. Stress can also bring feelings of tenseness, shortness of breath, difficulty in swallowing and even chest pains. Stress breeds mood swings, lack of enthusiasm, increased worrying, pessimism and irritability. It can make you 'hyper', rushing aimlessly about like a squirrel in a cage, or sluggish and listless. You may also become increasingly nervous and suffer from irrational fears and anxieties. None of these symptoms will help you to deal with the problems in your relationship.

Stress may cause behavioural problems, such as a withdrawal from family life or increasing dependency on 'comfort foods'. Scientists now know that chocolate in particular contains chemicals which enhance our natural 'feel-good' hormones.

Bingeing on chocolate or chips is unlikely to harm anyone except you, but drugs or alcohol are a different matter. Different drugs have different effects, so nobody can generalise. Alcohol is more consistent. Heavy drinking, especially drinking on one's own, leads to irritability, selfishness, jealousy, uncontrolled anger and violent behaviour. Turn, if you can, to the biscuit barrel rather than the sherry or gin bottle.

Here are some stress-busting strategies which have worked for us, our friends and our clients. You can probably devise others that work for you:

o Write down what you are thinking and feeling and what is upsetting you. Then make the page into a paper dart and see how far it will fly.

o   Talk to a friend about your problems. Even if your friend can offer nothing but sympathy, the intellectual exercise of expressing your problem in a way that your friend can understand can give you a lead to solving it.

o   Recognise what is causing you stress. Face up to it and try to remove it from or reduce its impact on your life.

o   Put the reason for your stress into context. Is it really as important as you first thought? Try asking yourself: 'In the terms of the history of the world, is this really so earth-shattering?' or 'Will I still be worrying about this in five years' time?'

o   Try and look at situations and events in a positive rather than in a negative way. Sometimes the mere idea of doing this is so farcical (try seeing the positive side of your car breaking down on the dual carriageway, in the rush hour, in the rain, on your birthday and you'll see what we mean!) that you burst out laughing anyway. All the same, the optimist with a half-full bottle is happier than the pessimist with a half-empty one.

o   Try and predict when a stressful event is likely to occur, so that you can prepare for it and deal with it more effectively. This is *not* the same as waiting in fear and dread for the worst to happen!

o   Manage your time more efficiently – prioritise. People under stress often feel overwhelmed by the sheer logistics of getting through a quite normal day. Split the day's activities into small, manageable chunks. Then decide which chunks can wait. Unmade beds never killed anyone.

o   This is probably a bad time to get a puppy, because all puppies trail stress behind them like Andrex, but make the most of any pets you may have. Walk the dog longer and farther than usual, and enjoy the uncritical affection. Stroke the cat (this is said to lower blood pressure and is in any case pleasurable for both of you). Consider giving a home to a kitten; they are less dependent than puppies and it is hard to feel tense with a kitten purring on your lap or chasing a leaf in the garden.

o   Do something you might not normally do. Visit a stately home, gardens or museum. Take a one-day course in something new – aromatherapy, perhaps, or china painting. Hire a horse or a bike and go for a ride; or book a session on the police skid pan.

o Rosy's Home Stressbuster Kit – a long, luxurious bath, with a family of plastic ducks, bubbles in the form of bath foam *and* a glass of champagne, scented candles, Mozart on the hi-fi and the *Times* crossword – works for her. You could have a lot of fun finding out whether it worked for you.

o Take a large, squashy foam pillow and give it hell.

o Take control of your stress. Recognise it is there, and accept that you have to work within its restrictions.

19

Children

Your mantra here is: *you and your **spouse**, together or apart, will be parents for the rest of your lives.* This fact must affect your relationship with the other parent. You want to be able to attend school functions together. Your children must feel able to invite both of you to family weddings, etc, without worrying about possible 'scenes'. You may have stopped loving each other, but you and your ex must be courteous. After all, you may have colleagues at work whom you heartily dislike, but you manage to be civil on a day-to-day basis. Is it so hard to do the same with someone you once loved to distraction?

You do not need to read many books about **divorce** to realise how harmful marriage break-up can be for children. You are bound to go through a bad patch. Reassure yourself that this is temporary. Talk to some couples who have been divorced for several years if you don't believe us.

Breaking the news

Try to do this together. Work out beforehand what you want to say, and keep things positive. Children tend to blame themselves for their parents' marriage break-up, and lie awake wondering what they have done.

With younger children, stress that this is a problem for adults (we know one mother who said cheerfully, 'It's a grown-up thing, like a mortgage' and her child, who had tuned into many heated discussions of the family mortgage, understood instantly), and not in any way their fault.

Older children will want to be consulted. They may have clear ideas about which parent they want to live with, and when they would like to see their other parent. As they grow older, children develop quite busy social lives of their own and contact arrangements should fit in with these.

Children might live with one parent for a while, then move to the other. We know of a boy who, after a couple of years with his mother, moved in with his father because the secondary school in his father's district had better facilities. He went home to his mother and sister at weekends and had friends in both localities. This seems to us most sensible, and it is to both parents' credit that he felt able to do this.

Some practical points

You have probably thought about all these for yourself, but in case any of them slipped your mind:

- When handing over the children for **contact**, be nice. It doesn't cost anything to say excitedly, 'Here comes Mummy/Daddy to take you out!'.
- Encourage the children to exchange letters, e-mails and telephone calls with your ex between visits.
- When you talk to your children about your ex, resist the temptation to put the boot in. The children love you both and can do so without being asked to take sides.
- Go easy on the presents and cosseting. Apart from the fact that money is likely to be short, all the trips and treats in the world will not compensate for the break-up of a family. Kids are not stupid. We know of an 11-year-old girl who accepted all the blandishments of her previously violent mother with a shrug, saying 'I'll take anything she gives me, but she can't buy me'.
- Friends and local support groups can be a big help. We know of families who regularly hire a minibus for shared low-budget outings and other activities.
- Make your children's friends welcome in your home. It doesn't cost much to provide squash and biscuits.

○ Keep in touch with grandparents and other relations. It's unfair to deprive your children of half their relations because you no longer get on with your former **spouse**.

○ Arrange child-minding (a babysitting circle among neighbours is one low-budget solution) and get some social life for yourself. Being a one parent family can be dreadfully claustrophobic and an evening class or dance session will do you good.

Always tell the children's school what is going on. Teachers are used to marriage break-up and will make allowances for any lack of concentration or behavioural lapses.

Court orders concerning children

If you and your **spouse** can agree sensible arrangements for the children, you should never need to go to court at all because there is no dispute. However, for the record, the courts can make four types of orders, known as Section 8 Orders because they come under section 8 of the Children Act 1989. These orders are:

○ **Contact Order** – where the **non-resident parent** is applying for 'visiting rights';

○ **Residence Order** to say which parent the child is to live with – the old word was to have *custody*;

○ **Specific Issue Order** – an order of the court about a particular question which has arisen in relation to a child, and on which the parents disagree. This may concern religion, health, schooling, etc;

○ **Prohibited Steps Order** – an order of the court to prevent something from happening without the court's consent, such as taking a child out of the country.

However, Children Act applications are emphatically not a DIY matter. Unless the matter is a dire emergency (in which case you should see a solicitor at once), disputes over children are best resolved amicably. We strongly urge you, before rushing into litigation, to try **mediation** with a view to arriving at whatever solution is best for the children.

Some real life 'behaviour' particulars

> He spent her money and slugged her and killed her canary bird, and told it around that she had cold feet. (O Henry.)

'Divorce particulars' are a bit like that – a blend of pathos and bathos. All these sample particulars are adapted from real-life **petitions**. We have omitted the really harrowing ones; you really would not want to know about the lady whose husband chained her up and forced her to watch while he pierced his own penis with a veterinary needle, or the husband who had to rescue his little daughter from a violent and sadistic mother. Here, however, is a real-life extract from a petition Rosy drafted in 1993, which we still find amusing – because the **Respondent** is now the manager of a large DIY store.

> The Respondent embarked on home improvement projects which always went wrong. He put nails through water pipes, built shelves that fell down and made a garden bench which collapsed under the **Petitioner's** mother during a family barbecue. The Respondent bought a new bath in a sale and put it in the bathroom but did not install it, with the result that for a year the entire family had to wash in the kitchen sink.

The Particulars below are examples only. You would not need more than half a dozen. More would be overkill.

Financial mismanagement

Throughout the marriage the **Respondent** acted in an irresponsible way with regard to the **parties'** finances and would often neglect to provide money for the household expenses, leaving the **Petitioner** to take responsibility for this.

The Respondent was careless with money throughout the marriage and was unable to manage his finances, which was to the Petitioner's and the children's detriment. The Respondent was, however, able to finance a trip to *[place]* with another woman which cost in the region of £XXX.

The Respondent became increasingly mean during the marriage, culminating in the Respondent turning off the central heating during the whole of the winter, including the Christmas holidays, and refusing to allow any hot water to be used for baths, insisting that the Petitioner had a shower only once a week.

The Respondent did not conduct his finances as though he were a married man; the Respondent was very secretive about his financial affairs and spent money freely, but not for the joint benefit of himself and the Petitioner.

Drunkenness

Over the two years prior to the parties' separation, the **Respondent** drank to excess. This resulted in the Respondent becoming abusive towards the **Petitioner**, sometimes in front of the child of the family.

The Respondent is an alcoholic, but refuses to acknowledge that he has a problem. The Respondent often vomits and urinates on the floor of the **matrimonial** home. He is regularly brought home by the police, who have found him lying in the gutter. The Petitioner finds this unbearably humiliating.

As a result of the Respondent's drinking, there was a constant strained and tense atmosphere between the **parties**, which the children found disturbing and bewildering.

Throughout the marriage, the Respondent drank to excess resulting in him becoming physically and mentally abusive to the Petitioner.

Drunkenness *and* financial mismanagement

During the marriage, the **Respondent** drank cider or 'Special Brew' to excess, often five cans during an evening, to the extent that it affected his relationship with the **Petitioner**. The Respondent and Petitioner were both in receipt of state benefits, but the Respondent would put his enjoyment of drink first. This meant that at times there was not enough money to buy food.

Bad temper, violence and intimidation

The **Respondent** has an ungovernable temper and flies into a rage over relatively minor matters and disagreements.

On *[date]* the Respondent broke the **Petitioner's** nose, and on *[date]* he broke her collar bone. When, on *[date]*, he started beating up the child of the marriage, the Petitioner left home, taking the child with her, and went to stay in a refuge.

At the end of April, the Respondent lost his temper and pushed the Petitioner to the ground. When she picked herself up, he pushed her down again. This caused grazing and bruising to the back of the Petitioner's hip.

Over the years there were many episodes of violence. On one occasion the Respondent threw the Petitioner and their children out of the house in their night clothes. On another the Respondent grabbed the Petitioner by the hair. These are just two examples from many years of similar episodes.

The Respondent often intimidated the Petitioner. She recently threatened to smash the Petitioner's car, which she knows the Petitioner needs in order to get to work.

The Respondent has been violent towards the Petitioner. On [date], the Respondent, after placing a knife to his own stomach and threatening to kill himself, then grabbed hold of the Petitioner's throat with both hands and shouted repeatedly 'if I cannot have you nobody else is going to'.

Physical violence *and* sexual abuse

On [date], the **Respondent** became physically aggressive towards the **Petitioner** and had sexual intercourse with her against her wishes.

Serial philandering

The **Respondent**, in 14 years of married life, has had affairs with at least 10 women and boasted to his drinking companions about his sexual exploits, to the **Petitioner's** great distress and humiliation.

Sexual problems

The two **parties** have not had any sexual relations with one another for almost two years because the **Petitioner** feels unable to bring herself to have intercourse with a man who has had so many adulterous relationships.

Since [date], the parties' sexual relationship has been non-existent. The Petitioner tried resolving matters with the **Respondent**, but she refused to discuss the matter.

The Respondent makes unreasonable sexual demands on the Petitioner and has on several occasions attempted to persuade him to take part in group sex, to the Petitioner's great distress and embarrassment.

Neglect of children and family life

During a trip to *[place]* in *[year]* the **Respondent** failed to acknowledge their son's birthday. The child did not receive a birthday card or present, or indeed a telephone call, from the Respondent.

During the marriage, the Respondent has spent inadequate periods of time with his children, preferring to spend time enjoying his hobby of motor mechanics.

On at least three occasions during the marriage, the Respondent walked out on the **Petitioner**. During *[year]*, the Respondent left the Petitioner for a period of three days and did not inform the Petitioner of his whereabouts. The Petitioner was frantic with anxiety and the children were distressed and bewildered.

Until the Petitioner left the **matrimonial** home in despair, the Respondent worked late every evening and spent his weekends away from home, neglecting the Petitioner and refusing to discuss the possibility of spending more time together in an effort to save the marriage. He would never say where he was going to be, which worried the Petitioner because people would ring up and ask for the Respondent and she was unable to help; also he was unobtainable in an emergency.

The Respondent did not eat with his family or share in family life. In the mornings he took the leftovers from the previous night's dinner to his work and ate them there at lunchtime; in the evening he either ate something at work or brought home a takeaway late at night. This hurt and embarrassed the Petitioner, who would have liked the Respondent to share meals and family life with her and the children, on the basis that 'the family that eats together, stays together'.

Verbal abuse

The **Respondent** was often verbally abusive towards the **Petitioner** and would undermine her confidence and cause her to feel depressed and unhappy.

The Respondent would often shout at the Petitioner and threaten her. He would tell her to shut up otherwise he would get angry.

Dishonesty

Throughout the marriage, the **Respondent** would lie to the **Petitioner** causing her great anguish and distress.

Jealousy and possessiveness

While the **Respondent** would go out and socialise on his own with his friends, he would not permit the **Petitioner** to do the same.

While on holiday in Spain during *[date]*, with the Petitioner's sister, the Respondent would not permit the Petitioner to go out with her sister.

The Respondent was obsessively jealous and refused to permit the Petitioner to have any friends of her own or any social life, interests or pursuits outside the **matrimonial** home.

Mild unreasonableness

Throughout the marriage, the **Respondent** was selfish and inconsiderate towards the **Petitioner** and took little or no account of the Petitioner's wishes and feelings.

On or about *[date]*, the Respondent accused the Petitioner of taking him for granted and stated that he did not love the Petitioner any more.

The Respondent has repeatedly stated to the Petitioner that he wants his freedom.

Generally, throughout the marriage the Respondent has failed to treat the Petitioner with the respect, care and affection she was entitled to as his wife and as a woman.

The Respondent refused to allow the Petitioner the use of the family car to go to her evening classes.

The Respondent was a dirty and inefficient housekeeper, who frequently left piles of dirty laundry lying about.

The Respondent was threatening, domineering and patronising towards the Petitioner, with the result that the Petitioner constantly felt 'smothered' by her during the marriage. The Respondent constantly told the Petitioner that she was ashamed of him.

During the five months prior to the date of this petition, the Respondent has increasingly picked arguments with the Petitioner about petty matters such as domestic chores not done and being unable to find various items. These arguments have become increasingly heated and upsetting for the Petitioner who is concerned that the yelling and shouting will upset the children of the family.

The parties' sexual relations ceased some three to four months prior to the date of this petition.

Useful forms

Statement of Arrangements for Children

Statement of Arrangements for Children

In the		County Court
Petitioner		
Respondent		
	No. of matter *(always quote this)*	

To the Petitioner

You must complete this form
If you or the respondent have any children

- under 16

or

- over 16 but under 18 if they are at school or college or are training for a trade, profession or vocation.

Please use black ink.
Please complete Parts I, II and III.

Before you issue a petition for divorce try to reach agreement with your husband/wife over the proposals for the children's future. There is space for him/her to sign at the end of this form if agreement is reached.

If your husband/wife does not agree with the proposals he/she will have an opportunity at a later stage to state why he/she does not agree and will be able to make his/her own proposals.

You should take or send the completed form, signed by you (and, if agreement is reached, by your husband/wife) together with a copy to the court when you issue your petition.

Please refer to the explanatory notes issued regarding completion of the prayer of the petition if you are asking the court to make any order regarding the children.

The Court will only make an order if it considers that an order will be better for the child(ren) than no order.

If you wish to apply for any of the orders which may be available to you under Part I or II of the Children Act 1989 you are advised to see a solicitor.

You should obtain legal advice from a solicitor or, alternatively, from an advice agency. Addresses of solicitors and advice agencies can be obtained from the Yellow Pages and the Solicitors Regional Directory which can be found at Citizens Advice Bureaux, Law Centres and any local library.

To the Respondent

The petitioner has completed Part I, II and III of this form
which will be sent to the Court at the same time that the divorce petition is filed.

Please read all parts of the form carefully.

If you agree with the arrangements and proposals for the children you should sign Part IV of the form.
Please use black ink. You should return the form to the petitioner, or his/her solicitor.

If you do not agree with all or some of the arrangements of proposals you will be given the opportunity of saying so when the divorce petition is served on you.

D8A - w3 F.P. Rule 2.2(2) (Form M4)(5.95)   1

Part 1 - Details of the children

Please read the instructions for boxes 1, 2 and 3 before you complete this section

1. **Children of both parties** *(Give details only of any children born to you and the Respondent or adopted by you both)*

Forenames ——————— Surname ——————— Date of birth ——

(i)

(ii)

(iii)

(iv)

(v)

2. **Other children of the family** *(Give details of any other children treated by both of you as children of the family: for example your own or the Respondent's)*

Forenames ——————— Surname ——————— Date of birth ——— Relationship to —

Yourself   Respondent

(i)

(ii)

(iii)

(iv)

(v)

3. **Other children who are not children of the family** *(Give details of any children born to you or the Respondent that have not been treated as children of the family or adopted by you both)*

Forenames ——————— Surname ——————— Date of birth ——

(i)

(ii)

(iii)

(iv)

(v)

2

Part II - Arrangements for the children of the family

This part of the form must be completed. Give details for each child if arrangements are different.
(if necessary, continue on another sheet and attach it to this form)

---

4. | **Home details**   *(please tick the appropriate boxes)*

(a) The addresses at which the children now live

(b) Give details of the number of living rooms, bedrooms, etc. at the addresses in (a)

(c) Is the house rented or owned and by whom?

Is the rent or any mortgage being regularly paid?   ☐ No   ☐ Yes

(d) Give the names of all other persons living with the children including your husband/wife if he/she lives there. State their relationship to the children.

(e) Will there be any change in these arrangements?   ☐ No   ☐ Yes   *(please give details)*

3

5. **Education and training details** *(please tick the appropriate boxes)*

(a) Give the names of the school, college or place of training attended by each child.

(b) Do the children have any special educational needs? ☐ No ☐ Yes *(please give details)*

(c) Is the school, college or place of training, fee-paying? ☐ No ☐ Yes *(please give details of how much the fees are per term / year)*

Are fees being regularly paid? ☐ No ☐ Yes *(please give details)*

(d) Will there be any change in these arrangements? ☐ No ☐ Yes *(please give details)*

4

DIVORCE AND SEPARATION

6. Childcare details   *(please tick the appropriate boxes)*

(a) Which parent looks after the children from day to day? If responsibility is shared, please give details

(b) Does that parent go out to work?   ☐ No   ☐ Yes   *(please give details of his/her hour of work)*

(c) Does someone look after the children when the parent is not there?   ☐ No   ☐ Yes   *(please give details)*

(d) Who looks after the children during school holidays?

(e) Will there be any change in these arrangements?   ☐ No   ☐ Yes   *(please give details)*

7. Maintenance   *(please tick the appropriate boxes)*

(a) Does your husband/wife pay towards the upkeep of the children? If there is another source of maintenance, please specify.   ☐ No   ☐ Yes   *(please give details of how much)*

(b) Is the payment made under a court order?   ☐ No   ☐ Yes   *(please give details, including the name of the court and the case number)*

(c) Is the payment following an assessment by the Child Support Agency?   ☐ No   ☐ Yes   *(please give details of how much)*

(d) Has maintenance for the children been agreed?   ☐ No   ☐ Yes

(e) If not, will you be applying for:
   • a child maintenance order from the court   ☐ No   ☐ Yes

   • child support maintenance through the Child Support Agency?   ☐ No   ☐ Yes

5

USEFUL FORMS

8. **Details for contact with the children** *(please tick the appropriate boxes)*

(a) Do the children see your husband/wife?

☐ No ☐ Yes *(please give details of how often and where)*

(b) Do the children ever stay with your husband/wife?

☐ No ☐ Yes *(please give details of how much)*

(c) Will there be any change to these arrangements?

☐ No ☐ Yes *(please give details of how much)*

Please give details of the proposed arrangements for contact and residence.

6

9. **Details of health**   *(please tick the appropriate boxes)*

(a) Are the children generally in good health?   ☐ No   ☐ Yes   *(please give details of any serious disability or chronic illness)*

(b) Do the children have any special health needs?   ☐ No   ☐ Yes   *(please give details of the care needed and how it is to be provided)*

10. **Details of Care and other court proceedings**   *(please tick the appropriate boxes)*

(a) Are the children in the care of a local authority, or under the supervision of a social worker or probation officer?   ☐ No   ☐ Yes   *(please give details including any court proceedings)*

(b) Are any of the children on the Child Protection Register?   ☐ No   ☐ Yes   *(please give details of the local authority and the date of registration)*

(c) Are there or have there been any proceedings in any court involving the children, for example adoption, custody/residence, access/ contact, wardship, care, supervision or maintenance?

(You need not include any Child Support Agency proceedings here)   ☐ No   ☐ Yes   *(please give details and send a copy of any order to the court)*

7

Part III   To the Petitioner

Conciliation

If you and your husband/wife do not agree about arrangements for the child(ren), would you agree to discuss the matter with a Conciliator and your husband/wife?

☐ No   ☐ Yes

Declaration

I declare that the information I have given is correct and complete to the best of my knowledge.

Signed . . . . (Petitioner)

Date: . . . .

Part IV   To the Respondent

I agree with the arrangements and proposals contained in Part I and II of this form.

Signed . . . . (Respondent)

Date: . . . .

8

Client care letter

(name)
Solicitors

Client Care Charter

1. We aim to provide you with a friendly, prompt and efficient service.

2. We will treat your affairs with complete confidentiality, unless

    - we are required by law to disclose information to the authorities (which will arise, for example, if we become aware of money laundering); or
    - we have a professional duty to do so (for example, if there is a threat to someone's physical safety)

3. We will use our best efforts to:

    - return your telephone calls within two hours,
    - answer your letters faxes and emails by return,
    - see you within one working day if you want an appointment,
    - see you immediately if your case is urgent.

4. If we have given you an estimate, we will:

    - carry out our work for you at the estimated fee, subject to the conditions which the estimate states,
    - if the estimate is for a matter which, for any reason, is not completed we will charge you for the work already done, plus expenses incurred. Similarly, if you ask us to do further work outside the scope of the estimate, we will make an additional charge.

5. If we have not given you an estimate, we will charge you on a time basis at an hourly rate. If relevant, we set out below the hourly rate for the work we are doing for you. We charge for time in 6 minute units. Standard letters faxes and e-mails which we send and receive, as well as telephone calls and personal attendances, are therefore charged in multiples of 6 minutes with a minimum 6 minutes per item. Time spent in travel is charged at half the hourly rate, plus travel expenses. We also pass on to you expenses we incur on your behalf, for example court fees, search fees and so on. Where we provide non-legal services we will charge them at the rate for legal services, unless agreed otherwise. We can ask you for advance and/or interim payments. If we will be working for you over more than 6 months, we will update the costs information we have given you at not less than 6 monthly intervals.

6. If we hold money for you, we will place it in our general client account i.e. a separate bank deposit account we have for any money which belongs to you, the client - not to us. In the case of large sums held over a long period, we will open an individual account for you. If you request, and subject to the Solicitors' Accounts Rules 1991, we will pay you the interest net of basic rate tax.

7. If you have any complaint about our service, please tell us. You should speak first to (name). If you are still dissatisfied, you have the right to complain to the Office for the Supervision of Solicitors, Victoria Court, 8 Dormer Place, Leamington Spa, Warwicks, CV32 5AE, telephone (01926) 820082. We will give you a copy of our complaints procedure on request.

The person dealing with your affairs is: (name)

The hourly rate we will charge you is: £( ) plus VAT.

(address, tel no and email)

also at: 16, Wentworth Road, Aldeburgh, Suffolk, IP15 5BB
176 Hamilton Road, Felixstowe, Suffolk, IP11 7DU

Certificate of Entitlement to a Decree

NO:

IN THE .... County Court

BETWEEN   Petitioner

AND   Respondent

Certificate of entitlement to a decree

F.P. Rules 2.36(1)

The Court certifies that the petitioner has sufficiently proved the contents of the petition and is entitled to a decree of divorce on the grounds of the Respondent's unreasonable behaviour.

Date:

Take notice that the Court has fixed the   at   for the

pronouncement of a decree by a District Judge sitting at Ipswich County

Court, 8 Arcade Street, Ipswich, IP1 1EJ

Note: Unless the decree of any of the orders is opposed, it is unnecessary
for any party to appear at Court for the pronouncement.

The court office at Ipswich County Court, 8 Arcade Street, Ipswich, IP1 1EJ is open from 10:00am until 4:00pm on Mondays to Fridays. Tel 01473 214256 Please address all communications to the Court Manager quoting the number at the top right hand corner of this form.
Printed By ECOATES

D84A Notice of Decree Nisi date

Sample of Decree Nisi (behaviour)

NO:

IN THE .... County Court

BETWEEN   Petitioner

AND   Respondent

Before District Judge   sitting at   County Court

On the

The Judge held that

the respondent has behaved in such a way that the petitioner cannot reasonably be expected
to live with the respondent,

that the marriage solemnised on

at

between   the Petitioner

and the   Respondent

has broken down irretrievably and decreed that the said marriage be dissolved unless
sufficient cause be shown to the Court within six weeks from the making of this decree
why such decree should not be made absolute.

Notes

This is not the final decree. Application for the final decree (decree absolute) must be
made to the court. (*For guidance see leaflet D187 "I have a decree nisi – what must I do
next"*)

Appeals: showing cause why this decree nisi should not be made final (absolute) is not an
appeal against the decree nisi.

*If the decree was pronounced by a district judge and the respondent wishes to appeal, he or she must serve
notice of appeal and set down the appeal at this court within 14 days of the date of the decree nisi.

*If the decree nisis was pronounced by a judge and the respondent wishes to appeal, he or she must serve notice
of appeal and set down the appeal at the Court of Appeal within 4 weeks of the date of the decree nisi.

The court office at Ipswich County Court, 8 Arcade Street, Ipswich, IP1 1EJ is open from 10:00am until 4:00pm on Mondays to Fridays. Tel 01473 214256 Please address all
communications to the Court Manager quoting the number at the top right hand corner of this form.
Printed By ECOATES
Printed by R CHENERY   D29 Family Man1 D29 Report

Application for Directions for Trial

In the

County Court

No of matter

Between

Petitioner

and

Respondent

and

Co-respondent

Application for directions for trial (Special Procedure)   *F.P. Rules 2.24*

The petitioner   applies to the District Judge for directions

for the trial of this undefended cause by entering it in the Special Procedure List.

The petitioner's affidavit of evidence is lodged with this application.

Signed   [Solicitor for] the petitioner

Dated

If you write to the Court please address your letters to "The Court Manager"
and quote the **No. of the matter** at the top of this form.

The Court Office is at

and is open from 10am to 4pm on Monday to Friday.

D84 -w3 (12.98)

Affidavit

Affidavit by petitioner is support of petition under
section 1(2)(b) of Matrimonial Causes Act 1973

Family proceedings
Rule 2.24(3) (Form M7)

In the **County Court***

No. of Matter

*Delete as
appropriate

In The Divorce Registry*

Between Petitioner

and Respondent

Question	Answer
About the Divorce petition	
1. Have you read your petition in this case including what is said about the behaviour of the respondent?	
2. Do you wish to alter or add to any statement in the petition or the particulars? If so, state the alterations or additions.	
3. Are all the statements in the petition and the particulars, including any alterations or additions, true?	
4. If you consider that the respondent's behaviour has affected your health, state the effect that it has had.	
5. (i) Is the respondent's behaviour as set out in your petition and particulars continuing? (ii) If the respondent's behaviour is not continuing, what was the date of the final incident relied upon by you in your petition?	

D80B (7.95) *Printed on behalf of The Court Service*

Question	Answer

6. (i)   Since the date given in answer to question 5 or, if no date is given in answer to that question, since the date of the petition, have you lived at the same address as the respondent for a period of more than 6 months, or for periods which together amount to more than 6 months?
 	
(ii)   If so, state the address and the period or periods, giving dates to the best of your knowledge or belief, and describe the arrangements for sharing the accommodation.
[State: :
    • whether you have shared a bedroom;
    • whether you have taken your meals together;
    • what arrangements you have made for cleaning the accommodation and for other domestic tasks;
    • what arrangements you have made for the payment of household bills and other expenses.]	

About the children of the family 7. Have you read the Statement of Arrangements filed in this case?	
8. Do you wish to alter anything in the Statement of Arrangements or add to it? If so, state the alterations or additions.	

9. Subject to these alterations and addition(s) (if any) is everything in your petition [and Statement of Arrangements for the child(ren)] true and correct to the best of your knowledge and belief?	

I,   (full name)

of   (full residential
                                                      address)

                                                      (occupation)

make oath and say as follows:-

1.   I am the petitioner in this cause.

2.   The answers to Questions 1 to 9 above are true.

(1) Delete if the
acknowledgment is signed
by a solicitor.   3.   I identify the signature _____ (2)
(2) Insert name as it appears   appearing on the copy acknowledgment of service now produced to me marked "A"
in the acknowledgment of   as the signature of my husband/wife, the respondent in this cause.
service.
(3) Exhibit any medical
report or document on which   4.   I exhibit marked "B" a certificate/report of Dr. _____ (3)
the petitioner wishes to rely.

(4) Insert the respondent's
name of the respondent   5.   (4) I identify the signature _____ (2)
has already signed a   appearing at Part IV of the Statement of Arrangements now produced to me and marked
Statement of Arrangements   "C" as the signature of the respondent.

                               6.   I ask the Court to grant a decree dissolving my marriage with the respondent(5) on the grounds
                                     stated in my petition [and to order the respondent to pay the costs of this suit](6)
(5) If the petitioner seeks a
judicial separation, amend
accordingly.

(6) Amend or delete as
appropriate

            Sworn at   )
            in the County of   )
            this day of   20   )
            Before me,   )   _____

(7) Delete as   A Commissioner for Oaths
appropriate   Officer appointed by the Court to take Affidavits. (7)

USEFUL FORMS   153

In the   **County Court***

No of Matter

In the Divorce Registry*

Affidavit by Petitioner in Support of
Petition under Section 1 (2) (b) of
Matrimonial Causes Act 1973

Full name and address of the petitioner or of
solicitors if they are acting for the petitioner

Sample of Decree Absolute

NO:

IN THE .... County Court

BETWEEN   Petitioner

AND   Respondent

Referring to the decree made in this cause on the   whereby it was decreed that the marriage solemnised on the

between   the Petitioner

and   the Respondent

be dissolved unless sufficient cause be shown to the Court within six weeks from the making thereof why the said decree should not be made absolute, and no such cause having been shown, it is hereby certified that the said decree was on the   , made final and absolute and that the said marriage was thereby dissolved.

Dated:

Notes:

1.   Divorce affects inheritance under a will

Where a will has already been made by either party to the marriage then, by virtue of section 18A of the Wills Act 1937:
(a) any provisions of the will appointing the former spouse executor or trustee or conferring a power of appointment on the former spouse shall take effect as if the former spouse had died on the date on which the marriage is disolved unless a contrary intention appears in the will:

(b) any property which, or an interest in which, is devised or bequeathed to the former spouse shall pass as if the former spouse had died on the date on which the marriage is dissolved unless a contrary intention appears in the will.

2.   Divorce affects the appointment of a guardian.

Unless a contrary intention is shown in the instrument of appointment, any appointment under section 5(3) or 5(4) of the Children Act 1989 by one spouse of his or her former spouse as guardian is, by virtue of section 6 of that Act, deemed to have been revoked at the date of the dissolution of the marriage.

The court office at Ipswich County Court, 8 Arcade Street, Ipswich, IP1 1EJ is open from 10:00am until 4:00pm on Mondays to Fridays. Tel 01473 214256 Please address all communications to the Court Manager quoting the number at the top right hand corner of this form.
Printed By ECOATES

D37 Decree of Absolute (Divorce)

Sample letters

Letter to court enclosing divorce petition

Your address

Date
Chief Clerk
.... County Court
[*Address of county court*]

Dear Sir

Divorce

I am the Petitioner in this matter and I enclose:

Marriage Certificate
Divorce Petition x 3 [*x 4 if you are citing a* **Co-respondent**]
Statement of Arrangements for Children x 3 [*If your*
spouse *has already signed the Statement, add 'signed by the*
Respondent' here.]
Cheque for £180 *or* Application for Remission of Fees.

Please arrange for service on the Respondent [*if there is a*
Co-respondent, add 'and the Co-respondent' here] and return
one copy of the enclosed documents to me bearing the
Court's seal.

Thank you for your assistance in this matter.

Yours faithfully

Letter to court enclosing Application for Directions for Trial and Affidavit

Your address

Date
Chief Clerk
………………….. County Court
[Address of county court]

Case no: [You will have a case number by now: insert it here.]

Dear Sir

Divorce

I am the Petitioner in this matter and I am now applying for Directions for Trial. I enclose:

Application for Directions for Trial
Affidavit

Thank you for your assistance in this matter.

Yours faithfully

Letter to court asking for petition to be served by court bailiff

Your address

Date
Chief Clerk
.... County Court
[Address of county court]

Case no: *[If you have one, insert it here.]*

Dear Sir

Divorce

I am the Petitioner in this matter and I enclose:

Request for Bailiff Service
Cheque for £10 *[unless you qualified for remission of fees]*
Recent photo of the Respondent.

[Here you should add details of where to find the Respondent.]

Thank you for your assistance in this matter.

Yours faithfully

Letter to court asking for the Decree Nisi to be made absolute

Your address

Date
Chief Clerk
………………….. County Court
[Address of county court]

Case no: *[If you have one, insert it here.]*

Dear Sir

Divorce

I am the Petitioner in this matter and I wish to apply for my Decree Nisi to be made absolute. I enclose:

Application form
Cheque for £30 *[unless you qualified for remission of fees]*

Thank you for your assistance in this matter.

Yours faithfully

Useful contacts

Replacement marriage certificates

The Registrar General

General Register Office
PO Box 2
Southport
Merseyside PR8 2JD

Tel: 0870 243 7788
E-mail: certificate.services@ons.gov.uk

Courts and official forms

Department for Constitutional Affairs

Selbourne House
54 Victoria Street
London SW1E 6QW

Tel: 020 7210 8614
Fax: 020 7210 8740
E-mail: general.enquiries@dca.gsi.gov.uk

www.dca.gov.uk

Look in the local telephone directory under 'Courts' for details of your local court.

Court Service website

www.courtservice.gov.uk
This website shows most of the forms associated with family law.

Housing and property matters

Land Registry

HM Land Registry
32 Lincoln's Inn Fields
London WC2A 3PH

Tel: 020 7917 8888
Action line: 0870 908 8061
www.landreg.gov.uk

Land Charges Department

Land Registry Plymouth
Plumer House
Tailyour Road
Crownhill
Plymouth PL6 5HY

Tel: 01752 636 6000

Telephone searches: 01752 635 635
Fax: 01752 636 161

Telephone outline applications
England: 0845 308 4545
Wales: 0845 307 4535

Housing benefit

Your local council will have all the leaflets about housing
benefit, but you can also access:

Women's Link

Room 417
London Fruit & Wool Exchange
Brushfield Street
London E1 6EL

Tel: 020 7248 1200

www.womenslink.org.uk

'Women's housing advice in London.'

Council of Mortgage Lenders

Consumer Enquiries
3 Savile Row
London W1S 3PB
Information line (automated, solely to order leaflets)

Tel: 020 7437 0075

www.cml.org.uk

Ask for their free fact sheet *Assistance With Mortgage Repayments.*

Shelter National Campaign for the Homeless

88 Old Street
London EC1V 9HU
Helpline: 0808 800 4444 (24 hours)

www.shelter.org.uk

Lawyers

Finding a solicitor in your area

Yellow Pages under 'Solicitors'

Law Society of England and Wales
113 Chancery Lane
London WC2 1PL

Tel: 0870 606 6575

www.lawsociety.org.uk

Complaints about solicitors

Office for the Supervision of Solicitors

Victoria Court
8 Dormer Place
Leamington Spa
Warwickshire CV32 5AE

Helpline: 0845 608 6565 (calls charged at local rate)
It's open from 9 am to 5 pm, Monday to Friday. The lines can get very busy so they run a queuing system.

Website reached through Law Society (see above).

Community Legal Services

This body can provide you with a list of approved lawyers.

Tel: 0845 608 1122

www.justask.org.uk

They don't provide legal advice but they tell you where to look, and they will provide a list of law firms in your area.

Income support and other benefits

Department for Work and Pensions

(used to be the DSS – Department of Social Security)
Helpline: 020 7712 2171 (9 am to 5 pm Monday to Friday)
www.dwp.gov.uk

The website offers links with other useful benefit-related sites.

Tax matters generally

Inland Revenue

New working tax credit helpline: 0845 300 3900

Disabled Persons' Tax Credit

Inland Revenue
PO Box 145
Preston PR1 0YX

Tel: 0845 605 5858
Fax: 01772 239 794

www.inlandrevenue.gov.uk

Inland Revenue National Insurance Contributions Office
Benton Park View
Newcastle upon Tyne NE98 1ZZ

Tel: 0191 213 5000

Legal help and public funding

Community Legal Service

Selborne House
54–60 Victoria Street
London SW1A 6QW

Directory line tel: 0845 608 1122

www.justask.org.uk

Or through your local solicitor.

Children and the family

Solicitors Family Law Association

PO Box 302
Orpington
Kent BR6 8QX

Tel: 0845 758 5671 (calls charged at local rate)
Tel: 01689 850 227
Fax: 01689 855 833

www.sfla.co.uk

An association of over 5,000 solicitors who are 'committed to promoting a non-confrontational atmosphere in which family law matters are dealt with in a sensitive, constructive and cost-effective way'.

Child Support Agency

National enquiry line tel: 0845 713 3133
www.csa.gov.uk
There are branches in main DWP offices.

NSPCC – if children are in danger

The NSPCC have a free 24-hour national child protection line.

Tel: 0808 800 5000
www.nspcc.org.uk

Parentline Plus

('Because children come without instructions'.)
520 Highgate Studios
53–79 Highgate Road
Kentish Town
London NW5 1TL

Tel: 0808 800 2222
www.parentline.co.uk

Families Need Fathers

134 Curtain Road
London EC2A 3AR

Tel: 020 7613 5060
www.fnf.org.uk

'Keeping Children and Parents in Contact since 1974.'

The website has much useful information, including forms for downloading and their 'Rough Guide to Law'.

Gingerbread

7 Sovereign Court
Sovereign Close
London E1W 3HW

Tel: 020 7488 9300
Fax: 020 7488 9333
E-mail: office@gingerbread.org.uk

Free advice line: 0800 018 4318 (9 am to 5 pm Monday to Friday).

www.gingerbread.org.uk

'The leading support organisation for lone parent families in England and Wales.'

Advice, support groups, literature.

Grandparents' Federation

Moot House
The Stow
Harlow
Essex CM20 3AG

Helpline: 01279 444964 (10.30 am to 3 pm Monday to Friday).

www.grandparents-federation.org.uk

Advice, support and information for grandparents of children affected by family break-up.

Emergency help

Police

Usually listed in your telephone directory under 'Police'.

Solicitors

See 'Lawyers', above or try your local *Yellow Pages* under 'Solicitors'.

Local housing departments

Listed with your local council.

Women's Aid Federation

National helpline: 0845 702 3468

www.womensaid.org

'Working to end violence against women and children.'

Advice, support and temporary accommodation for women and children fleeing domestic violence.

Marriage guidance, mediation and other counselling

Relate

Herbert Gray College
Little Church Street
Rugby
Warwickshire CV21 3AP

Tel: 01788 573 241

www.relate.org.uk

'We provide counselling, sex therapy, relationship education and training to support couple and family relationships throughout life.'

There are nearly 100 Relate centres in England, Wales and Northern Ireland with 2,500 trained counsellors (look in your local telephone directory under 'Relate').

The website offers 'Advice online', 'Find your nearest centre' and useful links with other organisations.

UK College of Family Mediators

Alexander House
Telephone Avenue
Bristol BS1 4BS

Tel: 01179 047 223
Fax: 01179 043 331
www.ukcfm.co.uk

Help in finding a family mediator near you.

Family Mediators' Association

Grove House
Grove Road
Redland
Bristol BS6 6UN

Tel: 01179 467 180
E-mail: info@fmassoc.co.uk

www.fmassoc.co.uk

Websites reached via the Relate website

National Family Mediation (NFM)

NFM is a network of over 60 local not-for-profit family mediation services in England and Wales, offering help to couples who are in the process of separating or divorcing.

Westminster Pastoral Foundation (WPF)

General counselling services in the UK with over 30 years' experience of helping people in all kinds of distress.

Home-Start

Provides support, friendship and practical help to families with at least one child under five.

One Plus One

Monitors contemporary marriages and relationships, focusing on understanding the causes, effects and prevention of relationship breakdown.

National Family and Parenting Institute

An independent charity to provide a strong national focus on parenting and families in the 21st century.

Other useful helplines

Asian Family Counselling Service

Tel: 020 8571 3933

Family Crisis Line

c/o York Road
Woking
Surrey
GU22 7XH

Tel: 01483 722 533

Provides confidential phone support service for people experiencing any form of domestic crises or situation that causes them stress.

National Council for the Divorced and Separated

National Secretary
c/o 14 Abbots Drive
Hucknall
Nottingham NG15 6QW

Tel/Fax: 07041 478 120
E-mail: info@ncds.org.uk

www.ncds.org.uk

National Council for One Parent Families

Lone parent helpline: 0800 018 5026

www.oneparentfamilies.org.uk

Click on www.divorce.co.uk

They say:

'This site is aimed to help families manage their way through marriage breakdown, separation and divorce' – and we like their style.

Index

Notes

Notes

DIVORCE AND SEPARATION

Notes

Notes

Notes

Notes

Notes

Notes

DIVORCE AND SEPARATION